A Quiet Room

Statue of Founder: Jakushitsu Genko (1290-1367)

A Quiet Room

The Poetry of Zen Master Jakushitsu

ARTHUR BRAVERMAN

TUTTLE PUBLISHING

BOSTON • RUTLAND, VT • TOKYO

First published in 2000 by Tuttle Publishing, an imprint of Periplus Editions (HK) Ltd, with editorial offices at 153 Milk Street, Boston, Massachusetts 02109.

Library of Congress Cataloging-in-Publication Data

Jakushitsu Genko, 1290–1367.
    A quiet room : the poetry of Zen Master Jakushitsu / Arthur Braverman.
      p. cm.
    ISBN: 0-8048-3213-7 (pbk.)
    1. Zen poetry, Japanese. I. Braverman, Arthur, 1942– II. Title.
    PL792.J35 Q85 2000
    895.6'122--dc21   00-020087

Distributed by

USA
Tuttle Publishing
Distribution Center
Airport Industrial Park
364 Innovation Drive
North Clarendon, VT 05759-9436
Tel: (802) 773-8930
Tel: (800) 526-2778

JAPAN
Tuttle Publishing
RK Building, 2nd Floor
2-13-10 Shimo-Meguro, Meguro-Ku
Tokyo 153 0064
Tel: (03) 5437-0171
Fax: (03) 5437-0755

CANADA
Raincoast Books
8680 Cambie Street
Vancouver, British Columbia
V6P 6M9
Tel: (604) 323-7100
Fax: (604) 323-2600

SOUTHEAST ASIA
Berkeley Books Pte Ltd
5 Little Road #08-01
Singapore 536983
Tel: (65) 280-1330
Fax: (65) 280-6290

First edition
06 05 04 03 02 01 00   10 9 8 7 6 5 4 3 2 1

Design by Stephanie Doyle

Printed in the United States of America

DEDICATION

To the Memory of Three 'Good Friends' (*Good Friend, zen chishiki* in Japanese, is an expression for teacher in Zen Buddhism)

Abe Kirschner
Adrienne Stalman Assail
Ichiro Shirato Sensei

ACKNOWLEDGMENTS

Thanks to Neil Nelson, a special friend and wonderful poet, whose interest in my first draft of the early poems encouraged me to continue when confidence started to fail. Neil is greatly responsible for teaching me how to listen to and hear these ancient voices. Thanks to Tony Connor, who read through my early draft of the first half of this text. Tony, an accomplished poet, had little exposure to Asian poetry. His thorough reading and candid comments helped me in a way that no enthusiast for Asian literature could match.

Gene Smith of Wisdom Publications sent the manuscript to James Sanford. Professor Sanford's comments were invaluable to me as I revised the text. Robert Aitken, Roshi of the Honolulu Diamond Sangha, sent me copies of Nyogen Sensaki Sensei's renditions of some of Jakushitsu's poems; renditions which helped me rethink some of my interpretations of the less accessible poems. Aitken Roshi has always been generous with his time and effort and I am grateful.

Nobody has had to answer more questions about obscure passages in the Japanese text than my wife Hiroko, Her patience and perceptiveness have kept me going more than anything else. Finally I thank our daughter, Nao, for her comments to my readings of some of the poems. As her ear for the English language has developed she's become her Dad's teacher.

Contents

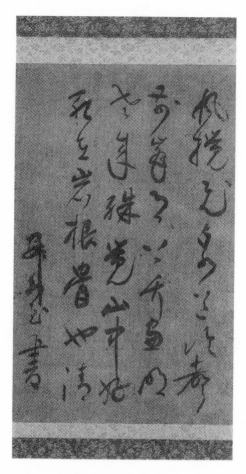

Calligraphy by Jakushitsu.

His most famous poem: Wind stirs waterfall…

(translation on page 2)

A Quiet Room[1]: Introduction

Zen Master Jakushitsu
(1290–1367)

In 1326 a ship from mainland China reached the shores of Japan in the province of Nagato.[2] Among the passengers were a Chinese Chan master named Ching-cho and a number of Japanese monks returning from the mainland. Ching-cho was a disciple of Ku-lin, the teacher most responsible for the spread of a literature and a style of Zen poetry that was to define learning in Rinzai Zen monasteries in Japan throughout the fourteenth century.

---

1. Quiet Room is one possible translation of the name *Jakushitsu* and the one that most represents the feeling his poetry gives me.

2. Most of the information on Jakushitsu's life comes from *Nihon no zen goroku*, vol. 10, edited by Iriya Yoshitaka (Tokyo: Kodansha Press, 1979); *Jakushitsu Genkō* by Ryûmon Harada (Tokyo: Shunjûsha Press, 1979); *Ōmi no shû Zuisekizan Eigenzenji Kaizanchokushi Enōzenji Jakushitsu Oshō Gyōjō* by Isshi Bunshu (Published in 1644); *Kokuyaku Eigen Jakushitsu Oshō Goroku*. The latter two manuscripts were copies from *Kokuyakuzenshûsōsho*, vol. 5 (Tokyo:Daiichishobô Press). Most of the information that Isshi Bunshu collected comes from an earlier biography written by (or credited to) Miten Eishaku, second abbot of Eigenji.

A Japanese monk on the ship gave his fellow travelers all the mementos he had received from his meetings with Chinese masters, said his good-byes, and slipped away into obscurity. There is no record of his whereabouts for the eight years following his return to Japan, and little is known of his life for decades after. He eschewed life in big cities where powerful lords and prominent monks sponsored the construction of large monasteries—places where new Zen literature was to flourish. Other than the recorded entries of his visits to their temples, nothing is known of his relationship with Ching-cho and Ching's teacher Ku-lin. His love for the art of verse, however, is evident in the poems he left us. The Japanese monk's principal teacher in China was Ming-pen, a recluse whose hermetic leanings were to influence the writings of his Japanese students. This Chinese master shunned the large religious centers on the mainland as did his disciple when he returned to Japan.

The Japanese monk's name was Jakushitsu. Like many Zen masters and Buddhist poets before him, he seems to have questioned the appropriateness of a man of Zen creating verse.[3] Though he may have given up poetry for long periods of time, he left us with enough poems to provide us a fuller understanding of his Zen than if we had only his letters and sermons to refer to. Whether he had developed a relationship with Ching-cho or Ku-lin, we can only guess. The style and subject matter in his poems leads us to believe that he was greatly influenced by Ku-lin at least indirectly. Because of his love of this art form, he left us descriptions of nature expressed with an immediacy that is the signature of good poetry. This apparently withdrawn Zen master came alive in verse—writing of friendship, loneliness, and death with a sensitivity that was both dynamic and vulnerable. And he managed this while maintaining an attitude that was both serious and playful:

> Alone
>   playing in this joyful leisure
> White haired
>   I face the green mountain

---

3. See, for example, William R. LaFleur, *The Karma of Words*, (Berkeley and Los Angeles: University of California Press, 1983), p. 8.

JAKUSHITSU'S LIFE

LIVING IN THE MOUNTAINS

Neither seeking fame
　　nor grieving my poverty
I hide deep in the mountain
　　far from worldly dust
Year ending
　　cold sky
　　　　who will befriend me?
Plum blossom on a new branch
　　wrapped in moonlight

Eigenji Monastery, is situated on Mount Zuiseki in a remote part of
Shiga Prefecture overlooking the Eichi River. It exemplifies the ideal of
rinka Zen. *Rinka*, meaning "under the forest," is contrasted with *sōrin*,
or "forest," and refers to the many temples located away from the large
centers of Kyoto and Kamakura. Rinka characterizes ideal Zen life, away
from the hustle and bustle of big cities and apart from the political pres-
sure of the powerful and wealthy. Eigenji, hidden amid mountains,
woods, and streams, reflects the natural beauty of rural Japan. The poet-
monk Jakushitsu, reluctant as he was to give up his life as a wandering
recluse, was lured away from the remote hills and backwoods of Japan
to settle in Eigenji when his aged bones could no longer easily carry him
from one mountain hermitage to another. Though Jakushitsu previous-
ly declined offers to take charge of two large *sōrin* or *gozan*[4] monaster-
ies, at seventy-one he became founding abbot of Eigenji. His close rela-
tionship with his disciple Sasaki Ujiyouri, ruling lord of Ōmi (present-
day Shiga Prefecture), who had the temple built for the master, and the
fact that Eigenji was away from the centers of political intrigue, Kyoto
and Kamakura, certainly influenced Jakushitsu's decision to finally set-
tle down as a teacher in a Zen monastery.

---

4. *Gozan*, or Five Mountains, is the name given to prestigious government-
ranked monasteries in Kyoto and Kamakura, another name for the *sōrin*.

The Ox-Herding Pictures are a series of ten illustrations accompanied by commentaries in prose and verse describing the stages of religious practice in Zen. The tenth picture, entitled *Entering the Marketplace with Giving Hands*, depicts one of the central themes in Zen: the final stage in the life of a Zen practitioner in which he shares his understanding with others. This is one way of looking at this period in Jakushitsu's life.

Roaming the mountains of Japan certainly seemed an intricate part of the lifestyle of this poet-monk whose most famous poem ends with the verse: "If I die at the foot of this cliff / even my bones will be pure." From the fact that Jakushitsu refused previous requests to serve as abbot of large monasteries we know that he must have struggled with this decision to take charge of Eigenji. What went through his mind at the time he made the decision, we can only surmise. This perceptive and elegant Zen master devoted five years to teaching and left a well-kept record of his letters, lectures, and, most important, some of the best Chinese poetry a fourteenth-century Japanese monk-poet ever produced. To better understand Jakushitsu's life and teaching, we must start with his early years, which, to borrow again from the Ox-Herding series, this time from the first picture in the series, can be described as "Searching for the Ox."

In 1303, when the thirteen-year-old Jakushitsu entered the Tôfukuji Monastery in Kyoto, Zen Buddhism was beginning to establish itself as a religion among the nobility and warriors of Japan. Yet the power of the older sects, Tendai and Shingon, was still to be reckoned with in the capital. Tôfukuji was a large Zen monastery founded by Enni Ben'en (1201-1280) in 1255. Along with a Zen meditation hall, it had facilities for Shingon and Tendai rites. Enni had received the seal of esoteric teaching in the Tendai tradition before traveling to China and completing his Zen training. He had also studied Confucianism for three years in Kyoto and was reputed to be one of the greatest scholars of his time. His reputation as a learned monk set the scene for an intellectual atmosphere at Tôfukuji that would help define that monastery through the ages. By the time the thirteen-year-old Jakushitsu entered Tôfukuji, along with the esoteric rituals, the practice of literature—eventually to be known as the literature of the Five Mountains (*gozanbungaku*)—played a major part in the activities of the monastery.

Jakushitsu was an unusually bright and sensitive boy. He did not enter Tôfukuji with the intention of devoting his life to religious pursuits. It was most likely the cultivation of academic learning rather than religion that prompted Jakushitsu's parents to entrust him to the care of the monks at Tôfukuji. Buddhist monasteries were best equipped to give him a sound education. Although he left Tôfukuji a few years later in search of a place where he could engage in a more concentrated Zen practice, during his time at the Kyoto monastery he felt the importance of a religious life and desired to become a monk. We can only speculate about the kind of education Jakushitsu received prior to his ordination into Zen monkhood from the direction his life took subsequently and from the scanty biographical information about his early years.

Jakushitsu was born in 1290 in the province of Saku (present-day Okayama Prefecture) into a branch of the Fujiwara family. The circumstances surrounding his birth as reported by his biographer resemble too closely other Buddhist hagiographies to be taken literally. According to his biographer Miten Eishaku, his mother had no difficulty giving birth, an auspicious sign. The room at the time of birth, Mitan said, was filled with a divine light, which caused the relatives present to conclude that the child would be exceptional.

The second entry in the biography describes an incident that took place when Jakushitsu was seven. A group of friends on a fishing excursion left Jakushitsu in charge of the catch. He thought to himself: "As trifling as these little creatures are, they are alive and one shouldn't take a life." To the group's consternation he set all the fish free. Nothing more is written about Jakushitsu's life before he entered Tôfukuji. One story pointing to the religious conversion leading to the boy's ordination tells of an invitation to an aunt's house sometime after he entered the monastery. The aunt prepared a meal for Jakushitsu including some boiled meat. The boy said to his aunt: "How can one who has entered a Buddhist monastery commit an act forbidden by the Buddha?" and refused to eat it.

His biographer writes nothing more of Jakushitsu's years at Tôfukuji other than to describe the events connected with his leaving the Kyoto temple. At fifteen, approximately two years after entering Tôfukuji, Jakushitsu was ordained. That same year, while traveling to Tanakami, a town in the province of Gô (present-day Shiga Prefecture), Jakushitsu saw a Zen monk absorbed in zazen.

The monk had just returned from Kantô (eastern Japan, including Kamakura). To quote Mitan, Jakushitsu was "secretly drawn to this practice and wanted to learn the way beyond letters." Apparently zazen wasn't a major part of the lives of monks at Tôfukuji, because Jakushitsu soon left the monastery in search of the kind of practice that this monk embodied. The practice of poetry, one of the central activities at Tôfukuji and one that was to mark Jakushitsu's genius in the future, was for him at age fifteen an indulgence that was keeping him from engaging in the life of a "pure" practitioner. This realization started to form as he journeyed through Tanakami, very near where he was to stay some fifty-five years later when he was drawn away from his life as a itinerant mountain monk to become the founding abbot of Eigenji. The period between Jakushitsu's departure from Tôfukuji until his installment as abbot of Eigenji saw him traveling through most of central and eastern Japan and parts of China.

Through a fellow monk at Tôfukuji, Jakushitsu learned of a teacher of rare quality, Yakuô Kenkô, who might fulfill the earnest young initiate's need for a severe champion of pure Zen. Yakuô was a disciple of Lan-chi Tao-lung (Rankei Dôryû in Japanese), a Chinese Zen master from Szechuan who had arrived in Japan in 1246. Soon after hearing this, Jakushitsu, together with his new friend, left for Zenkôji, the temple in Kamakura where Yakuô then resided. The young monk was intent on becoming a disciple of this Zen master. The evening before Jakushitsu arrived at Zenkôji, Yakuô is said to have had a dream in which "many saints had descended and a light bright enough to illuminate mountains and rivers was manifest." Hence the name Genkô, "Original Light," which Yakuô was to bestow on Jakushitsu.

Jakushitsu studied with Yakuô for the next few years, winning the master's respect and serving as his personal attendant. It was during this period, in his eighteenth year, that he had one of those profound experiences that defines the Zen school. He was attending the master when Yakuô suddenly became ill. Jakushitsu asked the master for a final poem. What he received was a slap on the face which acted as a catalyst for a *kenshô* , a glimpse into his true nature. There are two interpretations of the expression *"matsugo no ikku"* which I have translated as "final poem." One is "deathbed poem" and the other is "master's final word on Zen." It is difficult to know whether Jakushitsu thought that the master was dying when he asked for the final poem. If he did believe that Yakuô was dying and the master was only afflicted with a mild disease, then Jakushitsu, obsessed with receiving a final teaching from a man who was not in his final stages of life, was not really looking at *what is*. In that case the master's slap might have revealed to his disciple that he was living in a world of ideas and missing the present moment. If Jakushitsu was in the right state of mind, and it appears that he was, this realization would have a profound effect on him.

Jakushitsu remained close to his teacher until Yakuô's death in 1320. During this period, when he wasn't serving his master, he was training with teachers in accord with Yakuô's instructions. At age twenty Jakushitsu studied the precepts under a precept master, Eun, in Kanazawa for three months. This was followed by periods of study with three Chinese masters who came to teach in Japan. Yakuô, having received transmission from a Chinese master, wanted his prize student to study with the leading Chinese masters in Japan and was no doubt connected with many who resided there. Jakushitsu studied under the most eminent of them, I-shan I-ning (in Japanese, Issan Ichunei, 1247-1317), third abbot of the Nanzenji Temple during I-shan's final years. I-shan, one of the men most responsible for spreading the Chinese culture through the pre-*gozan* Zen world in Japan, had high praise for a poem Jakushitsu composed in his seventeenth year, "Bodhidharma in the Snow." This was the first mention of Jakushitsu's poetic skills in Miten's biography. I-shan most probably encouraged him to develop these skills. I-shan died in 1317 when Jakushitsu was twenty-eight, three years before the death of Yakuô. The year his teacher died Jakushitsu traveled to China, beginning a new chapter in his life. He was thirty-one years old.

Chung-feng Ming-pen (1263-1323), a well-known Chinese master who worked to restore Rinzai Zen, received visits from many Japanese Zen monks. He practiced in rigorous fashion and loved the quiet of secluded retreats. He insisted on faithful practice of zazen and well-regulated communal life, and many serious practitioners from Japan and China knocked on his brushwood gate. His lineage was referred to as the Genjû line and was one of the two important models for rinka Zen.

Jakushitsu stayed in China for six years, from 1320 to 1326. During that stay he visited many famous temples and met with many experienced masters. But his principal goal was to meet and study with Ming-pen. Little is recorded in Miten's biography of the time Jakushitsu spent with Ming-pen. But mention of one incident, which occurred at his first meeting with the Chinese master, is detailed, perhaps to emphasize Jakushitsu's determination to study with the renowned teacher.

> In the fourth year of Bunhô, the master was thirty-one years old. At that time he had heard of the Way of the priest Chûhô (Ming-pen) of Tenmoku—a flower that had shaken southern China. He sailed to China and climbed Mount Tenmoku. The sun was setting and the temple garden was covered with snow. With his two companions, Nen Kaô and Shun Donan, he stood in the garden, refusing to leave. Hô (Chuhô) wrote four characters on the master's arm, "come back following day."

The master immediately ran to the temple toilet, scooped a ladle full of water and washed off the writing. This story is followed by a list of places and teachers Jakushitsu visited in China.

Thirty years after Ming-pen's death, Jakushitsu composed a poem with a prose preface that demonstrated his great respect for his Chinese teacher. It was probably composed and brushed on a portrait of the late master. In the preface he begins: "If I am to comment on the old priest's presence, I would say the mountains, rivers, and the great earth are all illusion; form, emptiness, light and dark are all illusion; all the Buddhas of the three worlds are illusion." Playing on the word gen (illusion) which is the first character in one of Ming-pen's names, and the name of the school derived from his teaching, the Genjû line, Jakushitsu is suggesting that Ming-pen is all of these things, or that all is illusion in the face of his truth. Here is the poem that follows the preface:

Myriad virtues
    majestic perfection body

Even with the open sky for a tongue
    how can I describe him?

I make myself speak

"Since the time of the Buddha
    there has been only one"

Jakushitsu acclaims his Chinese teacher greatly here. Since this is a convention in a particular style of Zen poem, it cannot be taken alone as proof of his great respect for the Chinese master. The other piece of evidence, much more convincing, is Jakushitsu's style of Zen practice from the time he left Ming-pen. Ming-pen practiced a rigorous style of Zen in the seclusion of a mountain hermitage. He turned down the invitation of a Yüan dynasty emperor to come to the capital because he considered life in a cosmopolitan center incompatible with true practice. As was the case with most Chinese masters, Ming-pen advocated a blend of Pure Land teaching and Zen.

We have very few details of Jakushitsu's travels from the time he left Ming-pen. Like the Chinese master he stayed away from metropolitan centers and well-known monasteries, keeping his whereabouts unknown. His poetry abounds in references to a life of seclusion in the mountains and to rigorous practice:

> Green-tinged mountains
>   cut off worldly dust
>
> Moonlit ivy and
>   wind in the pines:
>   good neighbors
>
> Severe life
>   harsh practice
>
> No one visits my quiet dwelling

In his poetry and his sermons Jakushitsu refers to the Pure Land teachings with great respect. For him the true spirit of the Pure Land was no different from Zen. Whereas this attitude was quite compatible with the teachings of Ming-pen, it could not have developed under the influence of his Japanese teacher Yakuō, whose teacher Lan-hsi tried to purge Zen of influences and practices of other Buddhist sects.

Ming-pen died in 1323 at age sixty-one. Jakushitsu was thirty-four. He spent three more years in China visiting other teachers and historical spots where many of the old masters lived. He returned to Japan in 1326 to continue a life of wandering. Very little is known of Jakushitsu's travels from the time he arrived back in Japan until he agreed to become abbot of Eigenji some thirty-five years later.

One way of celebrating the new understanding arrived at by a disciple is through the presentation of a new Buddhist name. This milestone was usually accompanied by a poem brushed and composed by the teacher. When a Japanese monk trained in China, most, if not all, of his contact with his Chinese teachers was through the written word. Hence a poem brushed by a Chinese teacher was usually taken back to Japan and cherished by the disciple for the rest of his life. Jakushitsu went to China as Tessan Genkô, having received the name Genkô from his Japanese teacher Yakuô and the name Tessan from the Chinese teacher I-shan, whom he had served for two years in Japan at the request of Yakuô. On his return to Japan Jakushitsu carried with him, along with calligraphy and other presents from teachers he visited throughout his seven years in China, a poem brushed by Ming-pen. The poem was presented to him with the name Jakushitsu, given him by the master. According to his biographer, Jakushitsu gave all these possessions to his fellow travelers before leaving the ship in the Japanese port of Nagato.

After a brief stay in Misumi (present-day Shimane Prefecture), Jakushitsu disappeared for eight years, leaving his biographer to write: "hidden among the crags in the valleys, he remained far from society." Though Mitan was able to account for the monk's whereabouts for part of the seventeen years following this eight-year disappearance, Jakushitsu remained in relative obscurity, and few details of his life are known outside of the names of some places and temples he visited during a twenty-five year period after his return from China. And although the names of teachers he met and places he traveled in China appear in his biography, they are followed by the statement " as for the discussions with these teachers, Jakushitsu revealed them to no one." Jakushitsu seems to have made a conscious decision to remain inaccessible. His unconventional Chinese master, Ming-pen, whose love of solitude led him in his youth to go into hiding to avoid being appointed abbot of a monastery on Mount Tien-mu, was certainly a major influence on his decision.

During this twenty-five year period, Jakushitsu continued his life as an itinerant monk traveling through the southwestern part of Japan's main island, Honshû, staying in Bizen, Bitchû, and his home-town of Mimasaka (in present-day Okayama Prefecture) and Bingo (present-day Hiroshima Prefecture). He stayed in small rural temples, many of the Daikaku[5] branch of Zen to which his late teacher Yakuô belonged. His poetry is full of descriptions of the solitude and beauty of the mountains, valleys, and streams that surrounded him and of the animals who shared them with him.

Two major developments in the country at this time would appear to have been instrumental in keeping Jakushitsu from traveling anywhere near the capital or the religious centers of Japan. One was the continuation of a civil war that began in 1331 (Nambokuchô), and the other was the growing involvement the larger Zen monasteries were beginning to have with the government and the powerful warrior clans. The civil war started when the leader of the southern court decided to test the power of a then weak military council in an attempt to advance the waning empirial power. The struggle was to continue between the loyalists and the leading military clan, the Ashikaga, throughout the greater part of the fourteenth century. Military clans shifted allegiances so often and political intrigue was so common that it became difficult to see the possibility of any settlement ahead. The rising prestige of the Zen monasteries was to a great degree a result of the military government adopting the *gozan* (Five Mountains) system of ranking Zen monasteries, which led some of the larger temples to jockey for political power. Jakushitsu despised this mixing of politics and religion and remained as far away from it as he could. In his writings he didn't hide his disgust with the intrigue that was going on in many of the larger monasteries, but he rarely wrote about war. The following poem, however, is an exception. Composed toward the end of his twenty-five years of wandering through western Japan, it reveals his frustration with the war that plagued the country for a quarter of a century:

> Smoke of war everywhere
>   when will it end?
>
> Weapons in every temple and town
>
> A dream last night
>   even gold can't replace
>
> Briefly frolicking in nowhere land

---

5. The posthumous title given to Lan-hsi Tao-lung (Jpn., Rankei Dôryû). See Jakushitsu's zen below. For details on the life and teaching of Lan-hsi in English see Trevor Legget, *Zen and the Ways*, Trevor Legget (London: Routledge & Kegan Paul, 1978), pp. 40-61.

Attempting to remain reclusive in the Zen world does not always bring about the desired results. During this period Jakushitsu received invitations to take charge of at least two major monasteries, which he politely refused. But at age sixty-two he started to move away from the southwestern area to travel as far east as Kai (present-day Yamanashi Prefecture). No mention is made in the records of why Jakushitsu started his move east at this time, but the political climate in Japan again gives a hint of a possible motive. The constant fighting that had plagued the country for the last twenty-five years had escalated in the western provinces as an old feud between two of the Shōgun's chief generals and his brother and chief advisor, Tadayoshi, intensified. In an attempt to restrain supporters of his enemies in his brother's government in the west, Tadayoshi appointed his adopted son governor of the eight western provinces. It was at this time that Jakushitsu composed the poem "Smoke and war everywhere." This rare confession of his disgust for war makes one wonder whether he moved east to get away from the immediate fighting.

In another poem written at this time Jakushitsu asks his friend and fellow monk Reisō:[6]

> My mountain temple gate
>   extends to town
>
> How can I endure the daily hustle and bustle?
>
> I could buy a hoe for 100 copper coins
>
> Spend my remaining years
>   cultivating the green mountain.

In a second poem to Reisō, the poet laments the passing of so many old companions and asks if his own death might someday disturb Reisō's peace of mind. But it was Reisō who died first. Reisō had been in charge of the training temple at Myōzenji in Okayama. When he died, the monks there asked Jakushitsu to guide them through their

---

6. Reiso was the dharma heir to Jakushitusu's Japanese teacher Yakuō Tokken. He was the second abbot of Chōshōji in Kamakura, a monastery founded by Yakuō.

training season. Jakushitsu couldn't refuse the disciples of his old friend and agreed to join them for a three-month summer training period (*ango*). Although his poems expressed more and more the desire to live and die in the mountains, his sense of obligation seems to have worn his resistance down. His modesty only added to his appeal as a Zen teacher, and with his reputation grew a circle of new friends and disciples. When he spoke, disciples secretly recorded his words and treasured them.

Sometime during this period Jakushitsu made the acquaintance of the governor of Ōmi, Sasaki Ujiyori (1326-1370). Sasaki, a devout Buddhist, met Jakushitsu at Kuwanomi Temple where the master was temporarily residing. Sasaki was greatly impressed with the master's style of Zen and proposed to build him a temple at the foot of Mount Zuiseki along the Eichi River. Although in his new home Jakushitsu would be surrounded by the mountains and forests of rural Japan, where he felt most at home, he still would be a master committed to settling in one place. He did so, but from some comments in his letters it is apparent that it was not without some degree of sadness and even reluctance. The man who had spent most of his life wandering through the mountains of Japan and China, avoiding society and shunning public favor, was now to be founding abbot of a monastery with more than two thousand visitors passing through it during Jakushitsu's first year as abbot.

Jakushitsu's life at Eigenji was unassuming as ever. In his first year the young Bassui Tokushō, who had received dharma sanction from the Zen master Kōhō Kakumyō, visited the master. Bassui had been roaming the mountains of eastern Japan, advancing his practice in much the same way Jakushitsu had done years before, visiting teachers from whom he hoped to learn. Bassui had high standards for himself as well as for the teachers he met. Few teachers lived up to his standards, and he did not hesitate to express his disappointment with those who didn't. But he was not disappointed with Jakushitsu. His biographer relates that he was very impressed with the elegant simplicity of the master.[7]

The following year the master refused invitations tendered by the Shōgun Ashikaga Yoshiakira and the retired emperor Gokōgen to

---

7. See *Nihon no zen goroku*, vol. 11, Furuta Shōken, pp. 16 and 17.

become abbot of two well-known *gozan* head temples. He even went so far as to leave town so that he would not be present when the Shōgun's messenger came with an official request for him to be abbot of Kenchōji.

Five years after Jakushitsu took charge of Eigenji, he handed it over to his disciple Miten Eishaku. On the eighth month of the following year, 1367, Jakushitsu wrote his last will and testament and asked his two chief disciples to make sure his requests were carried out. On the first day of the ninth month of that same year he wrote his final poem and then passed away at the age of seventy-six.

JAKUSHITSU'S ZEN

Jakushitsu is officially affiliated with the Daikaku Zen lineage, inherited from his Japanese teacher Yakuō, who was a prominent disciple of Lan-hsi Tao-lung, a Chinese master. When he arrived in Japan in 1246 Lan-hsi quickly won favor from Japan's most powerful figure, the regent Tokiyori, who made him founding abbot of Kenchōji, the leading Zen temple in the military capital of Kamakura. Lan-hsi devoted his energy to purging Zen temples of the practices of other sects, particularly Shingon and Tendai, which he felt diluted the teaching of pure Zen in the Rinzai sect. He was successful in spreading this unadulterated Rinzai Zen throughout Japan, but not without the support provided by the government-sponsored monasteries and the unavoidable pomp and circumstance provided by the patrons from the ruling class.

Though Jakushitsu remained in contact with friends and fellow practitioners from the Daikaku line, the teaching of his Chinese master Ming-pen was far more suited to his temperament. Upon his return from China in 1326, Jakushitsu roamed the mountains of western Japan, visiting and staying with many of his old friends of the Daikaku Zen line. Even the temple he was to found, Eigenji, was considered to be in the Daikaku line. But Jakushitsu's greatest inspiration came from the eccentric Ming-pen, after whom the Japanese monk-poet seems to have modeled his life. Like his Chinese master, Jakushitsu spent many years wandering the mountains of Japan, refusing appointments to large monasteries. His own practice was quite austere. He refused to allow himself any possessions outside of the bare minimum needed for survival. In a letter to a Zen practitioner named Sai[8], he refused the present of a quilted coat. He wrote that he couldn't accept the coat because it was too valuable for an ordinary monk like himself to possess, and he returned it to Sai with his apologies.

Jakushitsu's biography and his letters to disciples and friends draw for us a picture of a humble monk who meticulously followed the teachings of the Zen patriarchs. But it is through his poetry that we can catch the true flavor of the heart-mind of the Mahayana, a mind that is broad enough to understand the possibilities of the unlimited while accepting the small, sometimes petty particulars of ordinary thinking. It was perhaps the need to express his feeling of the unlimited by way of the ordinary that compelled Jakushitsu to compose verse despite his own reservations about Zen practitioners writing poetry. In "Walking in the Mountains," one of four short poems on the topic of the "four dignified manners" (in Japanese, Shiigi)[9] he writes: "The sound of my voice bearing the pain blends with the sound of the river's flow." Jakushitsu's personal conflicts blending with the universal and hence coming into proper perspective is an implicit theme in much of his verse.

Jakushitsu sees his own view as small but recognizes it as one side of a more complete picture. In his poem "Buddha's Nirvana," he mistakes death for life: "Flowers that decorate valleys and mountains in spring/ I mistake for red leaves in autumn wind." While in his poems he identifies with the pain of a lone wild goose and the joy of a mountain bird, he recognizes the tentativeness of all these emotions and the mind that stands on firmer ground. In "Kingfisher" he writes: "Body rests on hazardous withered reeds / Mind remains in the depth of the waters bottom."

In his writings, particularly his poetry, he presents us with the extent of human emotions: longing, pain, anger, joy, and so forth, but there is always the opening for the unknown to enter: "I view a thousand peaks and push open the gate."

---

8. Sai Jisha of Hokugen. See p. 22 in the text for a poem and its prose introduction to Sai Jisha.

9. These are translated as walking, standing (sometimes as "being"), sitting, and lying down. They refer to the fact that the student should be mindful in these four positions, that is, in all positions, always.

TRANSLATOR'S NOTE

The poems translated here were written in Chinese or *kanshi* (Chinese poetry) as it is called in Japanese. The majority of Jakushitsu's poems are in the chüeh-chü (in Japanese, *zekku*) or quatrain form, with five- or seven-character line lengths. The second and fourth lines and occasionally the first rhymed in the earlier Chinese (they no longer rhymed in the Chinese or Japanese of Jakushitsu's time), and rules for tonal parallelism were followed. I refer the reader to any of the introductions to the kanshi works of Burton Watson[10] for a more detailed and authoritative discussion of the poetic form.

Following the course of most translators of Chinese and Japanese, I have made no attempt to include the rhyme patterns or to reproduce the syllabic patterns of the original in my translation. This is important to understand because the prose prefaces to some of the poems include statements about following the rhyme pattern of so-and-so's poem, a rhyme pattern that the reader will not see in translation.

I have tried to keep footnotes limited to those absolutely essential for understanding the poems so as to allow the reader to read each verse through with as little interruption as possible. When Jakushitsu uses an image from another text, many times from one of the popular kōan collections, I have quoted the significant passage above the poem rather than footnoting it.

My interest in Jakushitsu began when his work appeared in the record of another Zen master I had been translating.[11] My sketchy initial readings of his prose and poetry, led me to pursue his work further in order to better understand his Zen. After I had read and translated selections of his letters, sermons, and poems, it became clear to me that his real power as a teacher and as an artist was expressed through his poetry. To quote Iriya Yoshitaku, a translator and editor of Jakushitsu as well as of other Japanese and Chinese poets: "Jakushitsu's 'exceptional and superb works' surpass even those of the well-known contemporary *gozan* poet Chūgan Engetsu

---

10. For example: Burton Watson, *Kanshi: The Poetry of Ishikawa Jōzan and Other Edo-Period Poets* (San Francisco: North Point Press, 1990).

11. See the introduction to *Mud and Water: A Collection of Talks by the Zen Master Bassui*, (San Francisco: North Point Press, 1989), p. xviii.

(1300-1375), whose poems are impeccable in form but lack the depth of poetic feeling."[12]

I realize the difficulty in rendering living poems into a new language and don't pretend to be able to preserve the life of the original. I do hope to give readers a flavor for this unusual Zen master's life, and in the process encourage others more versed in the language and the poetry of this period to try their hands at these poems and improve on my attempts.

Arthur Braverman
Ojai, California
February 1999

---

12. See Heinrich Dumoulin, *Zen Buddhism: A History*, vol. 2, (New York: Macmillan Publishing Company, 1990), p. 204.

Part I[1]

Everyday Jui-yen called out to himself, "Master!" and answered himself, "Yes!"

Then he would say, "Are you awake?" and reply, "Yes!" And he would continue, "Don't ever be deceived by others!" "No I won't!"

[*The Wu-men Kuan*,[2] case 12]

OPENING GATHA (A RELIGIOUS VERSE)

Wu-yeh all his life called out
  "Don't be deluded"

Jui-yen simply said
  "Master."

In a deserted mountain
  sun shines through an ivy-tangled window

The sound of wind in the pines ceases
  and I enjoy a peaceful afternoon nap

---

1. The poems in this part were taken from *Nihon no zen goroku*, vol. 10, and *Kokuyaku Eigen Jakushitsu Ōshō Goroku*. See note 2 of the Introduction.

2. *Wu-men Kuan* (Japanese: *Mumonkan*), *The Gateless Gate,* is a collection of forty-eight cases (kōans) that appeared at the end of the Sung period (1229). The kōans in this collection are still widely used in Zen monasteries today. This collection has been translated into English more than any other. Two outstanding English translations still available are *Zen Comments on the Mumonkan* by Zenkei Shibayama (San Francisco: Harper & Row, 1974) and *The Gateless Barrier* by Robert Aitken (San Francisco: North Point Press, 1990).

Two Poems Written on the Wall at Kozôsan[3]

1

I acquired this hermitage a year ago

Cloudy peaks moon in the valley
    companions in withered Zen[4]

Come morning
    I descend the mountain road
        in front of this crag

What mountain rock will I sleep on next?

2

Wind stirs waterfall
    sending cold sound

Moonrise over the foothills
    shines its light on my bamboo window

Dearer with age
    these mountain ways

If I die at the foot of this cliff
    even my bones will be pure

---

3. There is a Rinzai temple called Konzôji in the mountains near the village of Ôta in the Town of Tantô in the district of Deishi in Hyôgo Prefecture. There was a place called Ôta Manor in the ancient province of Tajima, present-day Hyôgo Prefecture, where, according to notes in an old edition of the record of Jakushitsu, a place with the characters Konzô (pronounced *kin no kura*) existed. Konzôji is probably the temple mentioned in *Two Poems Written on the Wall at Konzôsan.*

4. Withered Zen is an expression indicating the destruction of body and mind; a state compared to that of a withered tree: the ideal Zen state.

On the thirteenth day of the ninth month I visited Taharamura village, spending the night in a thatched cottage. The monks accompanying me all went to sleep. Alone, I opened the window, gazed at the moon, and jotted down some old memories.

> Mid-autumn
> > in the year of the rat
>
> I stayed in a cottage
> > among the vines and mist
>
> Thinking back on my fifty-some years
>
> Have I ever known an evening
> > so deeply enchanting?

The Revered Itsu of Chōshū took a rock from his pocket. [It resembled] two mountains facing each other, as though a jewel were split. A white line ran through the center as though a waterfall were flowing there. A cold crag and an open cave and other forms, quite mysterious, bring with them thoughts of the deep mountains. I composed a chüeh-chü poem and presented it to him.

> Old friend
> > takes a rare object
> > > from his pocket
>
> Water falls off a steep cliff
> > a force from a thousand fathoms
>
> Reminds me of my visit to Mount Lu
> > many years ago
>
> Standing alone
> > in front of Shang-Feng Peak
> > > reciting verse

The National Teacher called to his attendant three times.
Three times the attendant responded. The National Teacher
said: "I thought that I had turned my back on you, but
alas! it is you who have turned your back on me."

[*Wu-men Kuan,* case 17]

*Ryū Jisha from Kansai is a man of excellent character and grace. He is a
prominent figure in the Zen world. Joining us in our practice in the moun-
tains, he maintained a simple life. Catching me unawares, he presented me
with a parting poem. I composed this poem in harmony with his to give
him encouragement on his journey.*

Many peaks
    after the snows
        air emitting green

Winter plums
    become ripe
        in the southern villages

Only this poem
    to send you on your way

Before the [National Teacher's] "three calls"
    fix your eyes and practice

A VISIT TO NAKAYAMA IN KIBI

Scenic spot
 thousand-year-old temple

Buildings
 amidst clumps of trees
  groves of bamboo

Scattered flowers
 buried along the path

Pheasant
 cries in a deserted mountain

The guest arrives
 before daybreak

Homeward journey trampling moon
 on the road

Who has graced these walls
 with an illuminating verse?

Ashamed
 as I add my own
  clumsy harmonizing poem

On the ninth day of the seventh month there was an envoy
from Chôshôji [requesting that Jakushitsu be installed
there as abbot]. Jakushitsu did not accept the post.

> [Eigenji kaisan En'ô zenji kinenroku,
> (Historical record of Zen Master En'ô,
> the founder of Eigen Temple),
> item for the year Kanôgennen (1350)]

For the Zen man In, messenger from Chôshôji

Messenger
    Messenger
        your mission is not to be mocked

You'll be honored throughout Zen monasteries

When your forthright speech touches our teacher

Grasshoppers
    bathed in autumn moonlight
        will cry deep into the night

WILD GEESE AMONG THE REEDS—[TWO POEMS]

1

Accustomed to sleeping in pairs by water's edge

How many rows fill the northern sky?

On a sand bar
  cold winter day coming to an end

And you perched alone—what deep sorrow fills your heart?

2

Late autumn
  cold frosty wind

Scanty rice and millet in the country fields of Ch'u

The geese are sleeping
  don't disturb them

They dream of flying home to the north country

Miso Jisha came all the way from Kenninji in the capital to visit me. We talked through the night and took pleasure in memories of our last ten years. Jisha returned to his temple in the province of Chô to check on the health of his teacher. He left two poems when we parted. In appreciation I sent him off with two poems that harmonized with the rhyme patterns of his.

1

Aging in this forest's edge
    no one to keep me company

How many dreams I've had
    of visiting the capital

I forgo this evening's zazen

Add oil to the lamp
    as we reminisce

2

Weary of tramping through worldly dust of fame and profit

In the shadow of a thousand peaks
    alone absorbed in the blessed ones

Suddenly an old friend knocks on my brushwood gate

Informs me once more of temple affairs

PRESENTED TO THE PRIEST CHIN AS HE DEPARTED ON A PILGRIMAGE

A man of Zen pays a visit
    I search for a verse to send him off

Secretly scrutinizing my withered heart

Not a phrase to offer him

The moon shines
    on deserted mountains
        autumn advances

Rain in Autumn

Look at the moon before you point or speak

Illuminating the sky
 an unstained round light

If your face doesn't possess the monk's discerning eye

You become blinded by evening rains of autumn

Two Poems Presented to Priest Reisô

1

I rise before dawn
 to the sound of wind in the pines

Cannot count old companions
 half must be gone

When will they bury my rotten bones?

And will this wild mound of earth
 disturb your leisurely dreams?

2

My mountain temple gate
 extends to town

How can I endure the daily hustle and bustle?

I could buy a hoe for a hundred copper coins

Spend my remaining years
 cultivating the green mountain

TWO CONNECTED POEMS FOR THE TEMPLE LIBRARIAN YÛ

1

We never exchanged letters or chatted

Only shared phrases of ancient masters
    nothing more was needed

Your old friend with his habitual sloth

Does not inquire into the details of your life

2

In the southeast the moon shines over the sea
    sky is clear

Arousing thoughts of eternity in noble men

You pluck out a tune on your stringless lute

Who can hear this wondrous sound in the wind?

CHRYSANTHEMUM FESTIVAL

Sun not yet up
    I sweep leaves
        stand at garden's edge

West wind blows on bamboo hedge
    hem of robe wet with dew

A mountain child appears
    picks a chrysanthemum

Tells me of today's festival

A Quiet Room

Narichika's Grave[5]

His life given for imperial cause
  only his name remains

Pathetic sight
  grizzled grave
    buried in moss

Ancient Nakayama
  still spring day

Fragrance of a flower in the rock
  calling the dark spirit back

Cherry Blossom Viewing at Muroyama

People playing in hills and meadows
  bright afternoon

I come upon a temple garden flush with flowers

A monk passes through a jeweled shadow of trees

Exquisite flowers thickly grown
  a bush warbler hidden in their midst

Embracing the stone pavement
  they color the moon over the mountain

Fluttering around the window
  they grace the incense smoke

A splendid scene
  rarely viewed since I've become old

Eyes drunk with this sight
  mind going mad

---

5. Narichika Fujiwara. Narichika (1137-1177) was a nobleman killed by Taira
no Kiyomori, leader of the Taira clan and virtual dictator of Japan from 1167 to
1185, for plotting against the ruler's regime.

A VISIT TO HATTOJI TEMPLE

Lone mountain dominating three provinces

White clouds cover a green peak

Summit soaring to great heights

Old temple nearly a thousand years

A monk meditates alone in a moonlit hall

A monkey cries in the mist in an old tree

Saying to worldly folk:

"Come here; free yourselves of karmic dust"

ON THE WAY TO KÔNE

Wondrous rocks
    curious crags
        blue mountain stream

White clouds
    red trees
        autumn's evening sun

I've traveled the mountains of Wu
    and visited the waters of Ch'u

But the joy of this beautiful journey has no equal

BUDDHA'S NIRVANA

Teacher of the three worlds enters nirvana

Humans and heavenly beings weep as one

Flowers that decorate valleys and mountains in spring

I mistake for red leaves in an autumn wind

Someone asked Chao-chou: "What is the Way?"
Chao-chou answered: "Outside the fence."

The questioner responded: "Not that. I'm asking about
the Great Way." Chao-chou said: "The Great Way passes
through the capital."

[From the Record of *Chao-chou Ts'ung-shen*]

SENDING THE HIGH PRIEST CHO
OFF TO THE CAPITAL

Eighth and ninth months
    scenic season

Geese cry
    once twice
        announcing autumn's coolness

Your passage clearly has public sanction[6]
    so move ahead boldly

"The Great Way passes through the capital"

---

6. *Kōken* is a kind of passport (giving one permission to travel). Here Jakushitsu
appears to play on the meaning, implying that his friend is advanced spiritually
and so is sanctioned to go to the capital.

RETURN VISIT TO DAIWAJI TEMPLE

A chance to visit this place once more

Late spring
    stillness of an enclosed garden

Flowers don't easily return to their trees

Snow effortlessly sticks to my head

Wind whistles through bamboo
    playing a previous dream

Tea made
    guest stays on

The next day
    wandering again
        staff in hand

In which mountain grove will I make my bed?

*In response to a request by the High Priest Yochoku of Juseiji Temple and
at the same time informing my seniors from this [Daikaku] line of my
refusal to accept the post [of Abbot of Kenchōji].*

An auspicious call
    twice brought to this wooded hill

I awaken from an afternoon nap
    open the bamboo door

Beckoned by the head of Dragon Peak[7] assembly

Please allow me to loaf on

---

7. The name of the tomb where Jakushitsu's teacher Yakuō was buried.

Offered to the recluse of the Ozawa Hermitage

Remembering the Zen Master Ozawa[8]
    in front of Great Warrior Peak[9]

I sit alone in zazen
    at the foot of Tranquil Heart Mountain[10]

You afflicted with disease
    and me with old age

Who knows how many more years we will see each other

---

8. The teacher of the recluse to whom this poem is written.

9. Taijihō, *sango*, or "mountain name," for the Zen temple Jikōji.

10. Anjininsan, a peak connected to Taijihō (Great Warrior Peak). See *Nihon no zen goroku*, vol. 10, p. 73.

ARTHUR BRAVERMAN

The seal of the Dharma is like the spirit of the iron ox.

[*Pi-yen lu*[11] (in Japanese, *Hekiganroku*), cases 38, and 69]

The iron ox is a symbol of strength and firm resolve. In ancient China, the Emperor Yu was said to have built a huge statue of an iron ox with its head in Honan Province on the southern bank of the Yellow River and its tail in Hopei Province on the northern bank as a guardian deity to prevent flooding from which the people suffered so many disasters.

The dawn of the sixth day of the seventh month of the year 1341 (the eighth zodiac sign, metal, at the hour of the snake), I dreamt I was dying and writing my death poem. I woke up and wrote it down.

How foolish
    shaping gold
        to cast this iron ox

Sleeping in a wooded hill
    lush with grass
        warm with mist

Turned fifty-two this year

Rejoicing at the sight of autumn growth
    despite no cultivation

On the evening of the twenty-fifth day of the sixth month in 1337 (the fourth calendar sign of Kemmu) at the hour of the cow, two verses came to me in a dream. I added two more.

Life is fleeting as dew
    as lightning

How can I vainly deceive myself
    seeking personal gain?

Taking things as they come
    I respond accordingly

Eating my fill
    and viewing the green mountains

Some friends got together, each expressing his desire. One said: "I want a lot of money." Another said: "I want to ride on a crane and fly through the sky."[12] A third said: "I want to be the governor of the state of Yang." And a fourth said: "I want to put one million five hundred coins around my waist, and ride to the state of Yang on the back of a crane."

[from the *Taiheikōki*]

In harmonized rhyme: An Evening Talk

Enemies from generations past

Gather one evening
    in a mountain hut

Angry words
    repeated reproaches
        regurgitating everything

Then coins tied around their waist
    they mount a crane
        and fly to the state of Yang

---

11. *Pi-yen lu* (Japanese: *Hekiganroku,* English: *The Blue Cliff Record*) is one of the most important kōan collections in Zen literature. A collection of a hundred cases (kōans) and commentaries originally compiled by Hsueh-tou Ch'ung-hsien in the eleventh century, it was composed in its present form in the twelfth century by Yuan-wu K'o-ch'in with his own commentaries and introductions to each case. Two English translations presently exist, the most complete rendition by Cleary & Cleary (Shambhala Press, 1978).

12. "Flying through the air on a crane" suggests the Taoist image of immortality. Together with the poem that follows, Jakushitsu is pointing to karma that is carried through generations. I can't figure out the allusion to Yang in both the poem and the quote.

LODGING AT SAIZENJI TEMPLE

Saizenji after the fire

Garden within the gate
     cold and silent
          like ash

Subdued sound of the Oi River

The green of soaring Mount Ran

Where only mountain clouds[13] settle in

Where laymen never go

Old master[14]
     secluded hermitage

Reviving old-style Zen

---

13. Mountain clouds symbolize wandering monks.

14. Musō Soseki, more popularly known as the National Teacher Musō (Musō Kokushi in Japanese.)

THOUGHTS OF A FRIEND

Mountain temple
    height of spring
        yet no one comes to visit

Garden vacant
    flowers fallen
        carpeting moss

I want to freeze this ever changing scene
    but I don't know how

The thoughts of the good friend I've been waiting for
    won't fade away

With age
    this secluded life suits me

Under a carefree cloud
    in the shade of a crag
        I make my bed

Waking from my afternoon nap
    with three cups of tea

I view the thousand peaks
    and push open the gate

Kuei-shan: "A day of gathering tea leaves and I hear only your voice. I don't see your form [you]. Show me your true form."

(Yang-shan shook the tea branches.)

Kuei-shan: "You've shown me your function [activity] but not your form [I still don't see you]."

Yang-shan: "What about you, master?"

(Kuei-shan was quiet for a while.)

Yang-shan: "Master, you've shown me your form but not your function."

[From a conversation while gathering tea, recorded in the *Ching-te ch'uan-teng lu*[15]]

GATHERING TEA

To the branch's edge
　　and the leaf's under surface
　　　　be most attentive

Its pervasive aroma
　　envelopes people far away

The realms of form and function
　　can't contain it

Spring leaks profusely
　　through the basket[16]

---

15. *Ching-te ch'uan-teng lu* (Japanese: *Keitokudentōroku*), the *Transmission of the Lamp*, is a compendium of Ch'an (Zen) biographies. There are two partial translations of this most important record: *The Original Teachings of Ch'an Buddhism* (New York: Pantheon, 1966); and *The Transmission of the Lamp: Early Masters* (Wakefield, N.H.: Longview Academic, 1990).

16. Jakushitsu probably studied the above conversation in which the Yogacarin Buddhist school idea of a consciousness beyond subject and object was recognized, and he wanted to equate the beautiful aroma of tea to this state of consciousness. It is beyond subject/object or form and function.

At the hour of the tiger (3 – 5 A.M.), in the winter of 1350, I climbed Kanayama Mountain to visit the worthy Kô,at his hermitage. I took a brush and composed these Shiigi [four dignified manners—walking, stopping, sitting, and lying down][17] *and wrote them down.*

WALKING IN THE MOUNTAINS

I walk near and far
    in the evening mist
        losing my way

Beside a valley river
    I stumble
        tearing my toe

The sound of my voice
    bearing the pain
        blends with the river's flow

STOPPING IN THE MOUNTAINS

I spend my days in grass-woven robes
    eating wild vegetables

A thousand peaks fill my eyes
    all day long

Don't remember how many times
    green's turned yellow

17. See footnote 9 in the Introduction.

SITTING IN THE MOUNTAINS

Rock slab seat
    legs folded
        sitting alone

Not loathing noise
    not savoring silence

The carefree clouds concur

LYING DOWN IN THE MOUNTAINS

High pillow by ivy vine window
    idling as I please

Wind blows
    breaking an old pine branch

Disturbing my sleep
    Damn it!

FOR THE HIGH PRIEST RIN

When I fraternize with you wise friend
    I forget my age

One evening
    thoughts stirring
        body tired
            fist for a pillow

I saw you clearly in a dream

Near the hearth
    listening to the snow
        we were talking Zen

FOR THE PRIEST JITSUÔ[18]
OF JÔMYÔJI TEMPLE

Daily
> I hear your praises sung
>> shining to the heavens

As usual
> old emaciated body
>> I lie in the mist on a crag

You called to duty
> third generation to Seirai[19]
>> Patriarch from the West

A heavy load
> for the shoulders
>> of one alone

---

18. Jitsuô was a disciple in the line of Rankei Dôryû, the teacher of Jakushitsu's teacher Yakuô. He was the fourth abbot of Jômyôji, one of the five major *gozan* monasteries in Kamakura.

19. The name of the pavillion where Daikaku's ashes lie. Jakushitsu uses *Seirai* to mean "Daikaku Zenji" (Patriarch from the West). Jitsuô, like Jakushitsu, is a third-generation disciple of Daikaku.

Bodhidharma, the Sixth Patriarch, arrived in southern
China in the eighth year of Futsû (527)....After meeting
the Emperor Wu of Liang, he proceeded to Shaolin
Monastery on Sungshan Mountain where he spent nine
years wall gazing (practicing zazen).... When Hui-k'o, the
Second Patriarch, first went to meet Bodhidharma, he was
refused admittance to the master's room. It was snowing
heavily, and Hui-k'o stayed knee-deep in the snow waiting
for the master to teach him. To show his determination, he
cut off his arm and presented it to Bodhidharma. The mas-
ter then admitted him to his room and conversed with
him. The subject of this interview is stated in case 41 of
the Wu-men Kuan.

Presented to the Elder Tôryû
in the Snow

Outside your hermitage snow piles high

Inside
    a monk alone
        practices zazen

If one of like mind were to visit

Would we talk of the year Futsû?

When I was returning from a pilgrimage at the end of the third month in the year 1348, I stayed with Hokugan Jisha. There I came across a beautiful poem. Expressing my feelings in verse harmonizing with its rhyme pattern, I wrote the following verses:

1

How far
    through these mountains
        have my straw sandals taken me?

Tired
    flying with injured wing[20]
        I return

Waiting
    as is my habit
        for a settled cloud to share my bed

Day comes to an end
    still I leave the brushwood gate open

2

The jewel under the black dragon's jaw
    is not easily obtained

More difficult yet
    to find a like-minded friend

Alone
    savoring the flavor of leisure

White haired
    I face the green mountains

---

20. A reference to the pre-Tang poet T'ao Yuan-ming's "Seeing the tired bird, I realized it was time to return."

Sai Jisha of Hokugen is a man of genius, dignity, and honesty. He possesses the character of the Zen monks of old. He has served me for a long time and been a true friend for many years.

In the winter of 1347 I planned to leave Jikô Temple and stay at Saiso and Myôzen Temples. Before finalizing my plans, Sai came to me asking permission to take leave. He wanted to return to the Gigu Hermitage to purify his practice. I didn't attempt to stop him, but rather applauded his aspirations. I sent him off with this poem.

Many years together
    our relationship firmly rooted

We pick up dry twigs
    boil water from the falls
        cook by the lonely shore

Your words soft but your heart resolute
    a true friend

You suspend duty
    forsake sentiment
        easily become intimate with the Way

Up high the pine gate closes
    you return to your old haunt

Looking down at the worldly
    they appear like floating dust

This old monk remains
    in a bamboo hut

Alone and enjoying the neighboring green mountains

LISTENING TO THE BUSH WARBLER

Don't mistake the crane's cry for the chirping of a bush warbler.

> [Lo-p'u Yüan-an (834-898), quoted from
> the *Ching-te ch'uan-teng lu*, vol. 16]

Can the crane's cry ever compare?

Deep in flower's shadow
    you play your mystic song

Its message present before you make the first sound
    and no one around who understands

Once again chasing the spring wind
    you pass through the low hedge

IN RESPONSE TO THE TEMPLE LIBRARIAN TEI'S VERSE, AND IN MATCHING RHYME PATTERN

You are the one to walk the patriarch's path

You've mastered meaning and know how to expound it

Don't say no one will understand you in a thousand years

We meet today
    our minds one

Mani pearl in Tathāgata storehouse[21]
    reflects light from heart to heart

Equipped with diamond sword
    blade sharp

We talk of the unborn
    deep into the night

The moon rises in the east
    in a valley under a distant peak

---

21. These images of the rarity of true dharma (*mani* pearl) hidden deep within us (Tathāgata storehouse) come from Yung-chia Hsuan-chiao's *Cheng-tao Ke* (Song of Enlightenment). The passages from which these images were taken are "The whereabouts of the precious *mani*-jewel is not known to people generally, Which lies deeply buried in the recesses of the Tathagata storehouse" (translation taken from D. T. Suzuki's *Manual of Zen Buddhism* [New York: Grove Press, 1960], p. 91). I have changed the "Tathāgata-garbha to "Tathāgata storehouse."

VISITING THE HERMITAGE OF
THE TEMPLE TREASURER NIN

What is this?
    you slipping off your robe
        hiding away

Choosing a Zen retreat
    in the shade of folded peaks

Like the shining nephew
    attendant to Ta-hui

In the end
    you'll follow the sixth-generation dharma heir
        to the Yang-ch'i sect[22]

IN GRATITUDE FOR THE VISIT OF
THE HIGH PRIEST TOTSUDO

Temple at the foot of a mountain
    in melancholy light of spring

A man of noble character with golden staff
    wipes away smoke and mist

Day is long on a deserted mountain
    how shall we spend it?

With only blossoms of a lone tree
    in front of the garden

---

22. This is a bit difficult to follow. Ta-hui is dharma heir to Yüan-wu coauthor of the *Blue Cliff Records* (*Pi-yen lu*). He is heir to the Yang-ch'i sect, one of the two major branches of the Rinzai sect during Sung China. Ta-hui may have referred to his dharma nephew Ying-an as "my shining nephew," and Jakushitsu is comparing Nin to Ying-an, who is the sixth-generation dharma heir of Yang-ch'i.

STOPPING OVERNIGHT AT SENKOJI TEMPLE

Ten years ago I visited an old friend here

Facing each other we held hands and talked

Here tonight again by chance I sleep in his old haunt

A cold moon reflects in the window
  bamboo branches flutter in the wind

IMPROMPTU POEM ON A COLD EVENING

Wind stirs cold woods
  a frosty moon shines

The guest arrives
  conversation enlivens
    we talk through the night

A skewer by the hearth
  baked potatoes go unnoticed

We listen quietly
  falling leaves tapping on the window
    sound of rain

FOLLOWING THE RHYME PATTERNS OF
THE HIGH PRIEST SHINGAN'S POEMS

1

I renounce the world once
    am a fool a hundred times

Sloth and torpor increase day and night

Still the peace of hills and valleys brings benefit
    in my final years

I watch guilelessly as others transmit the dharma light

2

Since leaving the world thirty years have passed

Face pale
    hair white
        aging in wind and frost

Autumn rain
    by window's edge
        in evening's blue light

Together we battle Zen's thorns and briars

3

Modern times
    dharma disappearing
        can any monk be revered?

So many running helter-skelter
    chasing after name and fame

You stand alone majestically
    a white cloud on a mountaintop

Answering the call of the Buddhas and patriarchs

SENDING DONSHUN OFF ON HIS TRIP TO SOYO[23]

My mind can make it to Dragon Peak[24]
    my body can't

Approaching my final years
    ghosts already nearby

I rejoice as you set out

In my place

    please sweep the dust from under the pagoda[25]

A ZEN PRACTITIONER FROM THE ASSEMBLY
IS SENT ON A PILGRIMAGE

Lin-chi studied Huang-po's Zen

He received sixty lashes
    like a pat with medicinal mugwort[26]

Now as you set out
    I offer this verse

Spring mountain after rain
    splashed with green

---

23. Sagami Province.

24. See note 7.

25. An expression that extols the teaching of Buttō. Jakushitsu is asking Donshun to carry on the teachings of Buttō.

26. An allusion to Lin-chi's enlightenment story from the *Record of Lin-chi*. The *Record of Lin-chi* is a record of the life and teaching of Lin-chi I-hsuan (d. 866), one of the great Tang China Zen masters. It is perhaps the most widely translated record of a Zen master. There are a number of English translations of this record. One is by Ruth F. Sasaki, published in 1975 by the Institute for Zen Studies, Hanazono College, Kyoto, Japan.
    Lin-chi was beaten on three occasions for no apparent reason by Huang-po —beatings which helped bring on his enlightenment experience. Before he had his enlightenment breakthrough he left Huang-po and went to Ta-yu, who called Huang-po's treatment of Lin-chi "grandmotherly."

WALKING IN THE MOUNTAINS ON A SPRING DAY

Hair on my head thinning
    twisted strands of silver thread

I may never know the coming spring

With bamboo staff and straw sandals
    I fully enjoy the rustic fields

How many wildflowers have I seen?

SPENDING THE NIGHT AT RYŪSEIJI TEMPLE

At the foot of White Cloud[27]
    banked by green pines

I pass the night in a monk's deserted quarters
    sitting until dawn

Dew washes the autumn sky
    the moon begins to rise

I make haste to greet my Dharma brother

---

27. Another name for Ryūseiji Temple.

I visited Shundonan. We talked through the night. In response to the poem he presented to me, I expressed my appreciation with this one of similar rhyme pattern.[28]

> We pass the night in elevated conversation
> > words that open our hearts
>
> This time
> > we tap with joy
> > > on mystery's door
>
> Body trembles
> > as I jump to the bottom of the abyss
>
> Return home
> > having snatched twenty-eight jewels
> > > from under the black dragon's jaw

So the Ino from the assembly of the Elder Jitsuô visited.[29] *He took out a verse that Jistuô had honored him with. I then presented him with this verse following the same rhyme pattern.*

> The silhouette of you swinging a golden mallet
> > kept in your sleeve pocket
>
> Peach blossom smile
> > willowy brows
>
> Unlike K'o-pîn
> > you're faithful to your Elder Hsing-hua[30]
>
> Returning to the foot of Jewel Mountain[31]

---

28. Shundonan's poem was in twenty-eight characters (four lines of seven characters each) expressing his joy and surprise that Jakushitsu braved the trek to his mountain hermitage. He writes of how they talked of old times and of his hope that Jakushitsu would stay longer.

29. The Ino is the monk who announces ceremonies and sermons by hitting a board with a wooden hammer. Regarding Jitsuô see note 18.

30. Hsing-hua, chief disciple of Lin-chi, had an Ino named K'o-pîn who disappointed him and had to leave the temple. Jakushitsu calls Jitsuô "So's Elder Hsing-hua."

31. Another name for Jôseiji Temple where Jitsuô resided.

KINGFISHER

When did you leave the deep forest?

Your vivid wings reflect in the pure pool

Body rests on hazardous withered reeds

Mind remains in the water's depths

WAGTAIL

Unconcerned with your brother's plight

You stand alone fluttering in the wilderness[32]

Bewitched by the sight of a butterfly's flight

Appearing to break the silence

FINAL DAYS OF SPRING

Boundless natural beauty already in decay

Lingering flowers still dance in front of the garden

Spring passes surely to come once more

But the old never become young again

Their remains buried in the green mountains

Calmly I place my deep feelings on a white cloud

Long quiet afternoon by the window
    seems like the passing of a year

Daily recitation of the Sûramgama sutra finished

I lean against my desk and nap

---

32. There is reference to the cry of the wagtail in *Hsiao-ya of the Shih-ching* (*Minor Odes of the Book of Poetry*) in which the cry of the wagtail sounds so desperate that the poet attributes the cry to its brother being in immediate danger. Jakushitsu is contrasting this with a silent wagtail. The meaning of the last two lines is anybody's guess.

For the Honorable Kô

Deep white clouds blanket the ragged roof

Grateful for this old Zen friend's visit

I send him off at the gate
    both of us silent

Standing under the shade of the tall pine
    lingering

Offered to the Honorable Seikô on his return from a visit to the High Priest Seizen

Amid bird cries and smiling flowers
your curiosity knows no bounds

Guided by a good teacher
    straw sandals in shreds

You have no equal among the throngs of monks

Staff in hand
    you visit me
        three times

Your Dharma mind clearer than the autumn stream

Your links to this world cooler than dead ash

Don't hide those destitute hands in your sleeves

Spread the light your teacher radiated

In mid-spring of 1318,[33] I spent ten days in the guest room of Tôzen Temple. During that time I would make occasional visits to Kagakuan Hermitage to see my dharma brother Shinkô. His unassuming elegance matched that of the ancients, Shan and K'o. Having made pilgrimages around the world for twenty years in this wretched condition, I'm ashamed that I still haven't attained a settled mind. Who other than I would visit you in chestnut-colored monk's robes and green straw sandals? For the occasion, I've composed these poems, to record my feelings.

1

Quiet, clear evening
    suitable to secluded inward thought

Moon illuminating ivy
    wind blowing through pines
        no one to claim them as their own

Impulsively I rap on the railing
    and give a protracted howl

Your only response, dear friend,
    the sound of a bell tolling at dawn

2

Spring
    marked by burned winter fields
        ferns sprouting from fertile land

Basket in hand I leave the temple grounds

Skillful means hidden up my sleeve
    not yet put to use

Ferns fist upright
    energy unfolding

---

33. The year 1318 must be a mistake because Jakushitsu would have been twenty-eight years old.

3

This life concealed in cold cliffs

Eyes watering uncontrollably
    mouth seeming glued shut

Mountain bird unconsciously reveals its mind

Chattering in the shade of overlapping peaks

4

The valley stream supplies tea kettle water

Mountain flowers sometimes enhance the fragrance of pagodas

Sitting on my torn cushion lacking nothing

I watch the evening sun hanging over the wood

In ancient times there was a monk who secluded himself
on Nan-shan Mountain. Once he couldn't find his kesa
(monk's shawl).

A monkey had stolen it, put it on, and did zazen on a
rock. Other monkeys from the pack saw this and all started
to imitate his zazen.

[From the *Hsueh-feng tung-shan wai-chi*[34]]

At the three gorges of Hatô a monkey's cry saddens me
Three crys and my sleeves are wet with tears.

[by Li Fang in the *T'ai-p'ing yu-lan*[35]]

MEDITATING MONKEY[36]

Monkey meditating on a flat rock

Attempting to reach beyond handholds[37]

Lonely reflection sinks to the bottom of Sorcerer's Gorge

Three cries stop the cool swirling stream

---

34. *Hsueh-feng tung-shan wai-chi* is Hsueh-feng's poetry collection in two
volumes from Sung China.

35. *T'ai-p'ing yu-lan* a poetry collection edited by Li Fang (925-996) and others.
Li Fang was a famous Sung official who was posthumously "canonized" as
Wen-cheng.

36. Perhaps this is the title of a brush painting.

37. The character for "to climb" (translated here as "handholds") can also stand
for "dependencies."

FOLLOWING THE RHYME PATTERN TO A VERSE
FROM THE HIGH PRIEST NIPPÔ

I've learned one thing in life
    how to be at leisure

And though I know the joy
    it's not easily put in words

A noble recluse of like mind

Staff in hand
    comes to visit me
        in these woods

*Your old dharma brother made a special trip to greet you, but you had
unexpectedly been called away. Though I thought I would return home
immediately, the sun had already set. I spent the night under the western
eaves in solitary meditation. Putting fifty-six characters together, I left my
impressions, humbly requesting you read them.*

To the High Priest, my dharma brother Gyoku Kan.

Old Veiled Dragon understands my mind

I make a special trip to your retreat
    entering the thickly grown wood

But staff in hand you had set out that morning

Taking refuge in a vacant hut
    I experience the depth of night

Your face appears in the mountain moon shining down on me

The wind in the pines purifies my ears
    speaking in your voice

I can truly say we met this time

The following day
    full of emotion
        I descend the green mountain

Rohatsu sesshin is a period of intensive meditation
commemorating the Buddha's [The Golden-faced One's]
enlightenment which is said to have taken place on
December 8. It is the most strenuous sesshin, an intensive
retreat, taking place during the coldest month and being
the most demanding on the participants who are encour-
aged to practice to exhaustion.

FOR THE SNOWS OF ROHATSU

Golden-faced One
    enlightened this morning

Unforeseen dread
    disturbing men and devas

I seek but a spark of the flame

Withered brushwood burning
    I gaze at the snow
        and sleep

In the *Record of Ryôshin* is a story of an old monk living in a hermitage who wrote the character for heart over the gate, on the window, and on the wall.

In the *Record of Chao-chou* is the story of the master [Chao-chou] visiting two hermitages. In each case the hermit raised his fist. To one Chao-chou said: "You have my consent"; to the other he said: "I don't agree."

After the Rhyme Pattern of Jisha Chu's verse[38] I offer to the master of Genkoan Hermitage

1

The ideogram for heart not written above the gate

Your fist held high
    neither estranged nor intimate

Some day Einichi and Kasuga[39]

Will illuminate heaven and earth
    with light to spare

2

In a chance meeting
    we were drawn to each other

Regretful how little I hear of your life

Our friendship in the Way for just a day

Surpasses ten years of casual fraternity

---

38. Jakushitsu probably saw Chu's poem to their mutual friend the master of Genkoan and used Chu's rhyme pattern to compose a verse to their friend.

39. These names apparently refer to places where the master of Genko once lived. Einichi translates as "wisdom sun" and Kasuga as "spring sun."

Old gimlet of Venerable Dragon's Peak [Jakushitsu]
Wind among the pines sweeps your white side locks
My plea: protect what is valued at a thousand gold coins
Auspicious Cloud [Buttō's dharma] in a state of disrepair

[High Priest Hogai's poem]

I was presented with a verse from the High Priest Hogai of Seikenji. I responded with four poems.[40]

1

Old gimlet of Dragon Peak[41]

Can anyone in this world be so dull?[42]

I have to laugh at myself today
    out picking chestnuts
        basket in hand

About to eat them
    I forget to remove the shells

2

Wind among the pines sweeps my white side locks

Deep in autumn
    my delicate body declines

Suddenly hearing of prosperity at my brother's temple

I stop tilling
    eyebrows lift with joy

---

40. Each of the four lines from Hogai's verses form the first line to one of Jakushitsu's four poems. Hogai was a disciple of Jakushitsu's teacher Yakuō Tokken (Buttō Kokushi); he was abbot of Seiken Yokokuji Temple in Suruga (in the city of Shimizu in Shizuoka Prefecture). Jakushitsu stayed at a small temple called Eianji in Shizuoka and Dragon Peak Mountain is the sango (mountain name) for Eianji. Hogai and Jakushitsu must have spent time together when they both lived in Shizuoka.

41. See note 7.

42. Hogai uses the phrase "old gimlet" to praise Jakushitsu's steadiness in practice (old gimlets stay sharp for a long time). Jakushitsu responds by comparing himself to an old gimlet that has gotten quite dull.

3

My plea:
    protect what is valued at a thousand gold coins

On the great turtle's[43] back
    three mountains soar

You evoke unrivaled teaching like the ocean's roar

Is there a monastery that wouldn't shudder at the sound?

4

Auspicious Cloud[44] in disrepair
    bring life to it

Naturally I turn to the old master of Great Turtle Mountain

Whose gate is never closed
    whose teaching is majestic

Wherever you come
    wherever you go
        who can stand in your way?

---

43. In the Ho Sea on Turtle Mountain (a mountain that according to legend is supported on the back of a great turtle) lives a hermit wizard. Another name for Hogai's Seikenji is Great Turtle Mountain (that is, its sango, or mountain name)

44. Written on the entrance gate to Buttō Kokushi's Ryuhoan Hermitage.

The head monk of Turtle [Valley] Mountain,[45] Etsuzan, visited me in the mountains and stayed for two months. We had pleasant talks, opening our hearts and looking deeply into questions of morality and virtue. When we parted I gave him this verse of fifty-six characters.

Elder Etsuzan of Turtle Valley Mountain

Talent soaring above ordinary men

Like Huang-po usurping noble Nan-ch'uan[46]

Or Ch'en Mu Chou secluding himself in an old temple[47]

With the *sangha's* sanction
    you're fit to express the master's truth

It's said your voice is so beautiful
    it startles ears

This time returning to your temple
    if you are chosen to lead

Revive the teachings of our declining sect

---

45. Turtle Valley Mountain is the sango for Jufukuji, founded by Myôan Eisai.

46. Huang-po was head monk in Nan-chuan's assembly. One day he took his begging bowl, held it up, and went into the dharma hall and sat in Nan-chuan's seat.

47. Ch'en Mu Chou was from Huang-po's lineage. He went to Mu Prefecture, secluded himself in Lunghsing Temple, and sold sandals to passersby.

Bright nephew [in the dharma] Kanmonrin had previously come to Ankokuji Temple entering my assembly. He was just fifteen years old then. Twelve years later we met at Eianji in Tōtōmi. Pleased to have the chance to be together again, we held hands and talked of old times. We weren't staying in the same subtemple but he often came to visit me. Stormy weather never deterred him. As summer turned to autumn the integrity of his aspiring mind became more and more visible.

This old monk, declining with age, once again desires to set out on a long journey in search of a hidden refuge. If we part today, we may not be able to meet again outside our dreams. Hence I can't control these feelings of regret. I compose this forty-character verse for him. I hope he will take it out and read it in the future when he thinks of me.

This phantom
　　this shadow
　　　　decides to truly hide away

In an autumn wind
　　you bid me farewell

Hotta Temple moon on a clear night

Ryūjusan Temple cloud in an evening sky

After you leave
　　who will think of me?

Only you!

Practice vitally
　　realize your resolve

Stir the teachings in this declining age

The attendant Zaiô visited my new dwelling in Nobe. We sat around the hearth all night in elevated conversation. When he left, I thanked him with this poem.

> Cut reeds
>> build a new dwelling on a deserted mountain
>
> You visit my remote retreat
>> filling me with gratitude
>
> We burn all the firewood
>> consume all the conversation
>
> Listen together to the cold rain beating on the window

A monk asks Pa-ling: "What is the Blown Hair Sword?"
Pa-ling says: "Each branch of coral holds up the moon."

[Pi-yen lu, case 100]

ADDED TO THE PLAQUE OVER THE ENTRANCEWAY AT KAIIN HERMITAGE

> The Buddha lightly presses his finger
>
> A great light radiates from the tip
>
> The hermitage master attains this samadhi
>
> From above
>> the moon holds up the coral's branch[48]

---

48. Case 100 of the *Pi-yen lu* is confusing enough by itself. Here Jakushitsu turns the last line on its head. In the *Pi-yen lu*, the moon, a symbol for enlightenment, is being held up by branches of coral (enlightenment reflected in all?). For Jakushitsu, the moon holds up the coral's branch. Does he mean enlightenment (the Buddha) will support the hermitage master? The sword, in the monk's question to Pa-ling, is the sword of Zen, sharp enough to cut a hair blown against it.

Sekikan, younger brother in the dharma, came to visit from far off and stayed for about ten days. We had delightful conversations around the hearth. I was deeply struck by his high moral principles. He parted leaving a poem. I thanked him with this verse in harmony with his rhyme pattern. I don't suppose it will bring a smile to his lips.

In a quiet cave
    frosty evening moon

In an ivy-tangled hut
    an old man's heart

The following morning
    you descend the mountain again

When will I hear you tap once more
    upon my door?

Two Poems Instructing Monks

1

Let me clarify the matter for you

No need to seek benefits

Wind mild
    sun warm
        warbler singing

Spring
    treetops rich with plum flowers

2

Zen is for the resolute

Body and mind molded into iron

Look at past Buddhas and patriarchs

Did any of them fritter their time away?

"Though now I am not in true nirvana, I tell you that I must enter nirvana."

The Buddha uses this skillful means to teach ordinary people. How is this accomplished? If he were to live long in this world, those with little virtue, the poor and the mean, attached to the five desires and immersed in a web of delusion--if they believed that the Tathâgata was always present, they would become haughty and lazy and unable to understand that it is difficult to meet the Buddha, and they wouldn't revere him.

[From *The Lotus Sutra,* chapter 16,
Revelation of the Life of the Tathâgata]

FOLLOWING THE RHYME PATTERN OF PRIEST JITSUÔ'S[49] CONDOLENCE POEM FOR PRIEST FUKUA

Old Buddha
    withheld his light
        mildly chastising monks

Don't say he's entered nirvana today!

His "Genju Zen"[50] discards personal self

Teaches reclusion
    true self not forsaken

Dust piles high on cushions of monks swayed by greed

Cherished writings of eminent teachers fill their letter boxes

Years pass
    our sect sinks deeper and deeper

We can but look to heaven and sigh

---

49. See note 18.

50. Genju Zen is the Zen line of the Japanese followers of Jakushitsu's Chinese master Chung-feng Ming-pen. Chung-feng worked to restore Rinzai Zen during the Yüan Dynasty (1260-1368). He loved quiet and seclusion and believed in rigorous practice. The Genju line was an important line in the Japanese Rinka (under the forest) Zen.

In 1361[51] I moved to a hermitage in the vicinity of Etsudani at the foot of Iitaka Mountain in the province of Omi.[52] Matsu Jisha was head monk under my old friend Kushitsu Roshi and was staying at Hyakusai Temple. He often visited my lonely hut. Though he frequently stopped by, he usually just sat facing me, not saying a word, then left. His noble countenance and grace were revealed in the expression of peace and harmony beneath his brows. I felt a secret joy when, in my old age, this friend of many years came to visit.

One day he told me that he was returning to his teacher's temple in the eastern province. I couldn't help but feel a growing regret at the thought of our parting. He took a piece of paper from his sleeve and asked me to write a few lines. He said that he would keep it as a remembrance until we met again. I quickly composed a twenty-eight-character poem and presented it to him.

With age this heart's become cast iron

Not even a verse reaches my tongue's tip

For you I will now put forth this token—

West wind and frosty leaves
    fill the valley
        fill the mountain

---

51. The year Eigenji was founded.

52. Present-day Shiga Prefecture.

A Brahman had become a monk. His hair whitened with
age, he returned to his native village. A neighbor seeing
him remarked: "Is that old man still alive?" "The same old
man but not the same," he replied.

[*Wu pu ch'ien lun*]

*Etsuunbō, a dear old friend, continued to appear in my dreams since our
parting some twenty years before. Then, one day, there was a knock on
my hermitage door. Holding hands, we talked of old times, enjoying our-
selves immensely. What's more, he presented me with a wonderful poem.
With great admiration, I thanked him with a verse harmonizing with the
rhyme pattern of his.*

Aged faces
        whitened hair
                years of separation

The same men of old
        yet not the same

This evening
        we pour out our deepest feelings
                endless pouring until...

The frosty moon at dawn
        sends beams of ice
                through my window

FOR MY JUNIOR DHARMA BROTHER SHŪ

Know that our sect is the wordless sect

Coming from afar what is it you seek?

Straw sandals on your feet
        west wind sharply blowing

The eighth month as ever
        is mid-autumn[53]

---

53. Autumn wind signifies impermanence.

SPENDING A NIGHT AT KÔYÔ TEMPLE

I spend a night on Mount Kôyô

The temple's founder was my friend

I bow three times to his statue in the alcove

A bush warbler cries in a green pine's shade

Master Yunmen's teachings:

1. permeate heaven and earth;

2. follow the waves and adapt to the currents;

3. cut through all streams [of delusion].

[App, *Master Yunmen*, p. 77]

NARUMI NO URA[54]

How many go east
    return west?

High tide makes walking the shore arduous

If you make the verse "Cut through the stream" your own

What can stop you from passing through the inlet gate?

---

54. A relay station on the old Tokaido road, in present-day Midori Ku in Nagoya City.

Range upon range of distant peaks, facing cliffs, pushing against barriers; if you linger in thought, holding back your energy, you will get stuck.[55]

[Yuan-wu's introduction to the *Pi-yen lu*, case 20]

TWO IMPROMPTU POEMS

1

Mind is Buddha
    image reflected in a mirror

No-mind is no-Buddha
    flame in ice

Rain passes
    clouds clear
        I lean on the railing and gaze out

Range upon range of distant peaks
    fold upon fold of green

2

I've never cared much for solemn discourse

Lazily I spend my days sleeping

Sound of a rat gnawing at the foot of my bed

Sunlight penetrates sparse bamboo
    shining on the edge of the eaves

---

55. A common Zen warning against conceptual reasoning.

Ta-mei Fa-ch'ang asked Ma-tsu: "What is Buddha?" Ma-tsu
responded: "This mind is Buddha." Later, hearing that Ma-tsu
had started using the phrase, "No mind. No Buddha." Ta-mei
said: "This mind is Buddha is good enough for me." Hearing
of Ta-mei's reaction, Ma-tsu said: "The plum fruit is ripe."[56]

[*Ching-te ch'uan-teng-lu*, volume 7]

GIVEN TO THE ZEN PRACTITIONER CHISOKU[57]

What is Buddha? This mind is Buddha

Plum Peak's fruit already ripe

Wind bitter
    rain sour
        smoke from the village ceases[58]

Sun sets
    the traveler at the crossroads is lost

OFFERED TO THE SCRIBE KEIGAN HÔ

My brother returns to Enrin Temple
    secluding himself

Though body frail
    still I bury myself deep in cloudy peaks

Winter again
    my life too descending

Nestled near the hearth
    listening to sounds of snow
        I remember you, dear friend

---

56. Ta-mei means "great plum."

57. The characters for Chisoku mean "insufficient knowledge."

58. Japanese plums are not eaten fresh because they are too bitter and sour.
The world, too, can appear bitter and sour, especially when one is confused.

> South of Hsiang
> > north of T'an
> Enough gold in between to fill a country
> A ferry boat under a shadowless tree
> No sage in the emerald palace[59]

> > > [*Pi-yen lu*, case 18]

Zui Jisha from Sagami came from far off to visit my mountain retreat. We spent the evening in delightful discourse. I am grateful indeed. He said he was returning to his hometown to pay respects to his teacher. He asked for a verse to guide him on his journey.

I am old and haven't used meter in a long time. At his request, however, I quickly put brush to paper and offered this verse.

> North of T'an
> > south of Hsiang
> > > a traveler wakes from a dream

> Staff in hand
> > you make your return journey of a thousand *li*

> Who knows that infinite scenery
> > defying depiction

> Beyond the green waters
> > beyond the blue mountains?

WRITTEN ON THE WALL OF SAIMYÔ TEMPLE

I came here last spring to view the cherry blossoms

And again today for the golden leaves of autumn

> Above the peaks
> > as though frozen
> > > white clouds stand motionless

> Shameful how
> > old and withered
> > > I still love idle play

---

59. Tan-yuan's poem from the *Pi-yen lu* appears to be describing a journey from this world (south of Hsiang and north of T'an) to the world of enlightenment (the ferry boat taking one to the other shore, nirvana, where there are no Buddhas, that is, no distinctions).

Kyûko Hermitage

Abandoned field
    at foot of mountain

Shovel and hoe thrown away
    thirty years ago

Pinecones
    an adequate meal

In the depth of ivy haze
    I shut my door and sleep

Advice to the High Priest Son

A seeker comes knocking on my brushwood gate

Wanting to discuss Zen's essence

Don't think me strange for not opening my mouth

In this village of falling flowers
    old warblers[60] no longer cry

Improvised in 1351

Smoke of war everywhere
    when will it end?

Weapons in every temple and town

A dream last night
    even gold can't replace

Briefly frolicking in nowhere land

---

60. The poet, in his old age, identifies with the warblers who stop crying in late spring.

In ancient times when the World-Honored One (The Buddha) was at Vulture Peak, he held up a flower to the assembly. All remained silent. Only Mahākākasyapa smiled.

The World-Honored one said: "I have the eye treasury of right Dharma, the mind of nirvana, the true teaching of formless form of no-form. It is not established upon words and phrases. It is a special transmission outside the scriptures. I now hand it to Mahākāsyapa."

[*Wu-men Kuan*, case 6]

A VISIT TO OLD VULTURE PEAK

Vulture Peak[61]
   ruined old temple

Yet spring
   brings visitors

A tree in front of the cliff
   two thousand years old

Its flower attracted Zūda
   his smile even fresher today

---

61. Vulture Peak is the name of the mountain in the neighborhood of the Indian city of Rājagriha where the Buddha gave his Flower Sermon. This was the initial mind-to-mind transmission of enlightenment in Zen, so important to its character.

Jakushitsu clearly didn't visit India. He is either creating this poem from his imagination or based on visiting a Japanese (or Chinese if he wrote this while in China) temple by the same name and conjuring up the rest. The Buddha gave his sermon almost two thousand years before Jakushitsu's time; hence the two-thousand-year-old tree.

Bodhidharma sat facing a wall. The second patriarch Hui-k'o had been standing in the snow. He cut off his arm, brought it to the master and said: "Your disciple's mind is not yet at peace. Please put it to rest." Bodhidharma said: "Bring me your mind and I will pacify it." The second patriarch said:

> I have searched for my mind but have not found it." Bodhidharma said: "I have completely pacified it."

[*Wu-men Kuan*,[62] case 41]

PRESENTED TO THE ZEN PRACTITIONER TA WHO WENT TO SHAOLIN TEMPLE TO PAY RESPECTS TO THE PATRIARCH (BODHIDHARMA)

The Great Way penetrates to the source

"Don't try to pacify your mind"

Old Ko's[63] body is still warm

Mount Sumeru
    standing in heaven
        is cold

---

62. See p. 20 in text.

63. The Second Patriarch Hui-k'o.

A Verse in Appreciation of the Candle Received from Jisha Ken

White clouds and green peaks
 near a rock-filled mountain stream

A shame
 you practiced Zen so many years
 behind closed doors

Flames strong
 flames weak[64]
 some soaring a thousand feet

I hope to see you carry the one light

Matching the Rhyme Pattern of the Shika[65] Kô

A guest comes
 delivers a beautiful poem

Each word like a jewel
 a lofty view

Ten thousand divisions
 a thousand distinctions
 all cut through

Amazed that the verse contains a blown hair[66]

---

64. Monmo, an alchemical term meaning "weak and strong flame," meaning tempered practice in this context.

65. A temple position. One who deals with guests and other nonresidents of the temple.

66. The blown hair cut by the sharp sword of Zen. See page 39 quote from *Pi-yen lu* and note 48.

> When [deluded thought] stops, when it has ended,
> a flower will bloom on an iron tree.
>
> [*Pi-yen lu*, case 40]

In the autumn of 1358 I stayed at the Nyoi Temple in Magori for the first time. I talked with a parishioner named Myôkai. Though it was our first meeting, we talked as old friends, animated in spirited conversation. The autumn evening is short. I left him with a poem and departed. When he takes it out and reads it, perhaps he will feel as though he were talking with me.

Lay follower Myôkai in the village of Ma

Householder surpassing homeless monks

Just follow the Way firmly
    carefully

Why assume a flower won't bloom
    on an iron tree?

The Zen practitioner Cheng of Hang-chou invited Chiu-feng, who had a temporary residence there, to join him in moon viewing. Chiu-feng expected dinner and arrived on an empty stomach. When Cheng ordered a boy to boil orange-peel tea and nothing else, Chiu-feng could only give the faintest of smiles.

[*Ch'an-lin seng-pao fu*, volume 19]

FOR MY DHARMA NEPHEW YOKU'S VISIT TO MY TEMPORARY RESIDENCE AT SEKITÔ

The wayfarer treads the snow and visits my temporary home

The moon shines on a cold window
    we sit opposite each other

Tea boils in an earthen pot
    first cup of spring

Not like Old Man Cheng's orange-peel tea

The attendant Jōgan Itsu is from the same dharma lineage as I. Coming to this mountain from far away, he joined us in arduous training on simple rations. Years passed, and now he informs me that he will leave shortly. He will return to his old teacher Kakuyū's retirement hermitage. My remaining years are few, and I fear that I won't have the fortune of meeting him again. Knowing that fills me with sadness. I compose these unpolished words as a farewell gift for his journey.

We lived three years together
    at the foot of this deserted crag

No time now to speak our minds
    no time to bare our hearts

Here I leave my final poem

If you return
    seek it in the mountain
        beyond that roof

On the summit above a thousand peaks
Stands a two-mat shack
An old monk in one half
    clouds in the other

[*Wu-ten hui-yuan*,[67] volume 17]

---

67. *Wu-ten hui-yuan* (Japanese: *Gotōegen*) is a revision of the *Wu-ten lu, the Five Records of the Lamp,* in twenty volumes. Revised in 1253, it consisted of the following five texts: *Ching-te ch'uan-teng lu* (Japanese: *Keitokudentōroku*), *T'ien-sheng kuang-teng lu* (Japanese: *Tenshō kōtōroku*), *Chien-chung ching-kuo hsu-teng lu* (Japanese: *Kenchū seitoku zokutōroku*), *Tsung-men lien-teng hui-yao* (Japanese: *Shūmon rentō eyō*), and *Chia-t'ai p'u-teng lu* (Japanese: *Katai futōroku*). These chronicles lay out the line of tradition starting with the seven Buddhas before Sākyamuni.

Tenkan, my elder dharma brother, came to this mountain to join me in a summer practice sesshin. Meeting day and evening, wandering together, sometimes sharing our deep feelings—reaching the state where "The crescent is impressed on the horns,"[68]

We could only throw our hands in the air and dance around. With the coming of the eighth month, I learned that he would return to his old residence. He showed me a beautiful poem, and I presented him mine, matching his rhyme pattern.

I walk to the horizon
    to the sea's edge and back

Clearing away reeds
    suddenly I come upon a secluded space

White clouds
    true friends of no-mind

I remember the ancient who shared his hut with them

PRESENTED TO HERMITAGE MASTER KYÔ

The mind is Buddha
    how crude!

No mind
    no Buddha
        no deliberation

Straw sandals trampling snow on barrier mountains[69]

Everywhere the smell of winter plums.

---

68. An expression indicating a level of attainment in Buddhist practice. In the record of Ming-pen, Jakushitsu's Chinese teacher, Ming-pen warns against getting stuck at this level of attainment.

69. A checkpoint between territories where few people live.

HARMONIZING WITH THE RHYME PATTERN FROM THE VERSE OF PRIEST REISÔ

Your thoughts absorbed in mountains deep
    face covered with ice and snow

In a world full of mundane minds
    wisdom like yours is uncommon

Oh how time passes by in vain!

Ten years since I've seen your stately figure.

The Temple Scribe Shigan often visits this mountain. His adherence to the principles of the Way is complete. What's more, he presented me with a beautiful poem. I can't praise it enough. I feel ashamed to try to follow it with one of my own. I won't dare follow the rhyme pattern, but rather just compose a short poem to repay him.

Don't ever show this to anyone. Just use it as paper for the front garden window or as a label for the bean paste jar and understand my true practice.

I'm old
    decrepit
        cast aside

Still you visit my hermitage

I search
    in vain
        for a phrase to see you off

And bid you farewell with a fist thrust in the air

SENDING OFF THE TEMPLE SCRIBE BOKU

Wiping away the Confucian seal

Smashing the Tathâgata Treasure House Jewel

Staff in hand
   strutting free
      through spring wind

Not far to go to this journey's end.

WATER MILL

In the light of a surging stream
   stands a turning mechanism

Like the Patriarch's turning of the Great Wheel
   at Tseng ravine

Passing from vessel to vessel
   its essence never varies

Washes from all beings
   dust of their dry minds

Framed plaque over the guestroom at the Ryûhô Hermitage.

SEIGOKEN (PURE LIFE ROOM)

A mountain tinged with green
   cuts off worldly dust

Moonlit ivy
   wind in pines
      good neighbors

Severe life
   harsh practice

No one visits your lonely dwelling

IMPROVISATIONAL VERSES IN MID-AUTUMN

1

In the garden
    with no one but the clear white moon

Golden autumn wind blows through my robe

I pick up fallen flowers
    their fragrance fills the earth

The sound of wild geese in the distance
    and my feelings too deep to fathom

2

Mid-autumn moon most cruel

Stirs this man's leisurely mind

In a year
    three hundred sixty nights

This evening
    one hour of moonlight turns me inside out.

LIVING IN THE MOUNTAINS

Neither seeking fame
    nor grieving my poverty

I hide deep in the mountains
    far from worldly dust

Year ending
    cold sky
        who will befriend me?

Plum blossom on a new branch
    wrapped in moonlight

FIRST WRITING OF THE YEAR HEIGO (1366)

1

Life in the mountains
    fresh as the first day of the year

The enlightened mind is in everyone

What's more
    the sky fills with congratulatory snow

A plum blossom opens
    one branch
        of five-petalled spring.[70]

2

One small protruding peak
    signifies spring

Throughout the world
    calm prevails

Don't fret about this mountain monk's white top

Since morning
    snow's covered the ten-thousand-year-old pine.[71]

---

70. Traditionally the first day of the new year was considered the first day of spring.

71. There is said to be a ten-thousand-year-old pine tree on Mount Tendai. Here Jakushitsu may be referring to the long life of the dharma at Eigenji.

STAYING AT KONGÔ TEMPLE

I often visit this neighboring temple

And talk incessantly with the priest
    through the night

Mountain village
    no evening drumming

Light at the window informs us of the dawn.[72]

WRITTEN ON THE WALL OF THE SHIMURA MOUNTAIN HERMITAGE

Valley stream flows to the world of men

Cloud over a crag floats to another mountain

I hear the faint cry of a wild bird

Sounds like the joy this rustic priest knows in his leisure

---

72. Many villages had drumming to inform people of the time.

Part II

The following poem is the first in a series called gōju, poems titled with Buddhist names (hōgō in Japanese) of both lay and monastic followers. The title usually consists of two Chinese characters and serves as a kind of springboard for the subject of the poem. Many, though not all, of the subjects relate to the recipient of the new name.

Kōgetsu (Cultivation Moon)

I chase away the iron ox[73]
    repeatedly whipping it.

No neglected field in front of this temple

Rain passes by my plow
    traveling beyond a thousand peaks

The jewel rabbit pushes the full moon
    sinking in the dawn.

---

73. The image of the iron ox traditionally represented resolve and strength (see p. 13 in this text). Here Jakushitsu appears to be using the image to characterize the mind that requires a firm resolve to conquer.

MUSAN (NO PRACTICE)

Here and now you know your faults
    drop them and be done with it

What is there to seek?

Child from the south with top knot

Journeys in vain through one hundred castles
    wandering toward the hazy waters[74]

KŌGETSU (MOON IN THE SOUND [INLET])

The vast river Ch'u
    splashes to the sky

The tide shakes Ch'ien-tang Sound
    unsettled through the night

A jeweled mirror reflects the cool light
    under ten thousand waves

From the beginning
    autumn's full moon
        lights up the heavens.

---

74. This poem refers to a parable from the "Entry into the Universe" (in
Japanese, *Nyuhōkaibon*) chapter of the *Garland* (in Japanese, *Keigon-kyō;* in
Sanskrit, *Avatamsaka*) sutra in which the child Zenzai traveled past 101 castle
[towns] and met 53 teachers in his search for enlightenment. See *Nihon no zen
goroku,* vol. 10, p.158.

Subhūti, master of emptiness
flowers rain on you; for shame
Snapping my fingers,
I scold you, Subhūti
Don't be deluded
for I will give you thirty blows

[*Pi-yen lu*, case 6]

TONGAN (RETREAT ROCK)

Like the people who fled the tyrant Chin
        you left all traces of this dusty world behind

Placing your shabby body under green pines

So alone
        no birds to bestow flowers

Refusing to let the master of emptiness live nearby[75]

---

75. Two ancient stories are alluded to here. One is of Zen Master Fa-jung who as
a student lived on Mount Niu-t'ou. It was said that birds dropped flowers on
him every morning when he meditated. After he met the Fourth Patriarch, Tao-
hsin, the birds no longer dropped flowers on him. The second is about one of
the Buddha's ten disciples, Subhūti, referred to in this poem from the Pi-yen lu.
    Subhūti was known for his meditation on emptiness. Once when he was prac-
ticing meditation the deities poured flowers down on him in praise of his deep
practice. Subhūti was not happy with the deities' show of admiration. Both sto-
ries point to the fact that both men had not reached true emptiness if flowers
could still be showered on them. In true emptiness who would be there to
receive the flowers?

Kuei-shan questioned his disciple Hsiang-yen about his original being before he was born. Hsiang-yen could not respond and implored his teacher to help him. When told he had to find out for himself, he searched in vain through his Buddhist texts. Finally he burned his texts and went into retreat, absorbing himself in Kuei-shan's question. One day while working in the garden, he heard the sound of a falling tile and was enlightened.

[*Ching-te ch'uan-teng lu*, volume 11]

CHIKUIN (HIDDEN IN BAMBOO [GROVE])

Yearning for your upright and empty mind

I built this hut even deeper in the mountains

Let's not carelessly throw tile at bamboo

I fear the dull sound will reverberate in temples

CHIKUDŌ (HERMITAGE SURROUNDED BY BAMBOO)

I think of the ancient master Hsiang-yen
    enlightened by the sound of a tile striking bamboo

In our Six Gate sect[76]
    we face the distant peak
        and cultivate the Way

Plucking leaves and searching for branches

Many return with nothing to show for it

---

76. The six gates are the eyes, ears, nose, tongue, body, and mind.

Sesshô (Woodcutter in the Snow)

Flapping in the wind
    fragments of empty flowers[77] scatter

Old man Lu
    ax in hand
        leaves through the brushwood gate

Feeling chilled to the bone from the severe cold

He returns with the rootless tree[78]
    over his shoulder

Besshô (Separate Sect)

Though free of the finger pointing to the moon

It's not Flower Sermon Zen

I have heard of a clay cow seeking
    counsel from a wooden horse

That is the Buddha's true transmission

---

77. Objects without substantial body; the snow giving the illusion of flower fragments.

78. One of the three objects that are nonexistent or impossible to obtain and which, according to the Wu-teng hui-yuan, the seven bright maidens requested of the deva T'ing-shih t'ien.

KANSÔ (PATIENT OLD MAN)

On his face
　　saliva remains[79]
　　　　like drops of rain

Near his ears
　　abusive language
　　　　like thunder's roar

A tranquil life of many years

How many white eyebrow hairs he has grown![80]

GATSUÔ (OLD MAN MOON)

He sits in a palace
　　high in the sky

Wind blowing through his half frosted hair

His light engulfs the universe
　　overlooking nothing

Both eyes a twinkle
　　getting brighter with age

---

79. He doesn't react to being spat upon.

80. There was an old belief that the hairs of one's eyebrows fell out if one taught anything false. Hence this last verse indicates that he is a true teacher.

The Fifth Patriarch Hung-jen realized he was coming to the end of his life and urged each of his disciples to compose a poem demonstrating his level of enlightenment.

Shen-hsui wrote:

> The body is the tree of wisdom,
> the mind a bright mirror in its stand.
> At all times take care to keep it polished,
> never let the dust and grime collect!

Hui-neng dictated the following:

> Wisdom never had a tree,
> The bright mirror lacks a stand.
> Fundamentally there is not a single thing—
> where could the dust and grime collect?

["The Story of Early Ch'an" by John R. McRae
in *Zen: Tradition and Transition*, p. 27]

KAN-Ô (MAN IN THE MIRROR)

Polish the pure platform of the mind

Old chestnut mirror facing you
   a blossoming flower shines
        from beginningless beginning

Illuminating your original face

You raise your snow white eyebrows and smile

KEIAN (REVERED RETREAT)

Discreet in all activities

Who would not revere him?

Head bent
    sitting alone in a thatched cottage

A hundred birds vanish[81]
    quiet spring afternoon

Then the Buddha sent a ray of light from the circle of white
hair between his eyebrows, illuminating the eighteen thou-
sand worlds in the eastern quarter. It reached everywhere
from Avici hell to Akanishthâ heaven.

[*The Lotus Sutra*, introductory chapter]

SAIHÔ (WESTERN PEAK)

Above the five heavens one lofty form
    soars alone

Dominating the eighteen thousand worlds
    in the eastern quarter

Without advancing one step I reach the summit

At this rustic monk's feet
    T'ung-hsuan-feng Peak[82]

81. See note 75.

82. Taken from a poem in the *Ching-te ch'uan-teng lu,* vol. 25, by the Chinese
monk T'ien-t'ai Te-shao who lived on T'ung-hsuan-feng Peak. He said that
T'ung-hsuan-feng Peak was the dharma in man's heart:

Over the crest of the T'ung-hsuan-feng,
The human world is no more.
Nothing is outside the Mind,
And the eye is filled with green mountains.

Quoted from John C. H. Wu, *The Golden Age of Zen,* (New York: Image Books;
Doubleday, 1996), p.180.

ETSUDÔ (HALL OF JOY)

When simple joys in daily life
    are not seen as slight

Lanterns and pillars
    smile their bright smile

Who understands this meaning
    first clarified some thousand years ago?

He who sits steadfast
    under the eaves appreciating
        the cool wind
            the cool moon

SÔTEI (ANCESTRAL GARDEN)

In front of the of the Patriarch's room
    the road is smooth

A thousand years pass in vain
    moss grows

Bright moon
    shines like snow

The Second Patriarch
    his arm severed
        still hasn't arrived[83]

---

83. p. 20.

Flying dragon in the heavens. It furthers one to
see the great man.

> [*I-Ching* (Book of Changes),
> Hexagon no. 1 Ch'ien (The Creative)]

Confucius says about this:

Water flows to what is wet, fire turns to what is dry. Clouds
(the breath of heaven) follow the dragon, wind (the breath
of earth) follows the tiger.

> [Wilhelm/Baynes, *The I-Ching*, p. 9]

KOUN (SOLITARY CLOUD)

Lone cloud
    unbound
        floats free

Swirling
    stretching
        spreading
            shrinking
                as it pleases

Laughing at those who follow the dragon

Alone it faces the depth of the old mountain
    returning to its true home

IUN (HAPPY CLOUD)

In this mountain I am joyful

Uncommonly clear and cool
    a familiar feeling

Though I lean on the railing
    looking out unhindered

I fear I may drift away
    following the dragon
        and turn to rain

UNSÔ (OLD MAN IN A CLOUD)

Unfolding and refolding in no-mind
    growing faint

A thousand peaks
    ten thousand valleys
        and how many years later?

You've long since ceased following the dragon
    and becoming rain

Your children and grandchildren naturally linger
    hanging from the heavens

RANAN (LAZY RETREAT)

Alone I do as I please
    excusing myself from all concerns

Brushwood gate tightly shut
    I pass my final years

When I meet people
    I forget to open my mouth

Don't worry
    I'm of no mind to raise my fist[84]

SEKISHITSU (ROCK CHAMBER)

Ten-foot square hut on a steep crag
    who would frequent this place?

Door and windows tightly shut
    covered in moss

Blue-eyed one at Mount Sumeru
    facing a cold wall

Golden-faced one at Magadha[85]
    secluded behind the gate of emptiness

---

84. See page 35, above.

85. According to the *Chu-fo yao-chi ching*, the Buddha secluded himself in a room in Magadha and entered samadhi. Magadha is the country where the Buddha attained enlightenment.

Ma-tsu and three disciples went moon viewing. Ma-tsu
asked what they were doing on this occasion. Ch'iu-tang
said: "I bring incense." Pai-chang said: "I bring my prac-
tice." Nan-ch'uan brushed his sleeve and left. Ma-tsu then
said: "Only Nan-ch'uan has transcended things."

[*Ching-te ch'uan-teng lu*, vol.6]

GETSUOKU (MOON HOUSE)

1

Before the moon is full
    you see its roundness in a flash

A grass hut turns into a jeweled tower

Even Elder Nan-ch'uan
    transcender of things

Knocks on the gate
    pushes the door open
        but can't enter

2

With a jade ax
    repeated shaping
        and who knows how many autumns[86]

A jeweled tower and golden palace emerge
    rarely matched craftsmanship

Even one whose discarded light and form

Must resign himself
    for the time being
        to remaining outside the gate

---

86. There is a Chinese myth that there are eighty-two thousand families living
on the moon who are there to mend the chipped parts.

GATSUSAN (MOON MOUNTAIN)

1

Fix your eyes on the fullness before the moon is full

Where the green mountains soar over its vast cool shrine

If you look toward the light reflected

Cloud enclosed
    mist covered
        myriad peaks manifest

2

Moon ring hangs high
    blue sky wide

Peaks piled
    like jewel clusters

Even Subhūti
    master of emptiness
        sits under a crag
            heart torn asunder

Lone monkey cries its last
    cold dawn

JIZAN (MOUNTAIN BRUSHED)

With a twist of your brush
    nature comes to life

A lone precipice
    juts to the heavens

See before you make a mark
    and

Mount Sumeru won't equal half its height

Junsô (Orderly Old Man)

Relating to others
    you don't flounder about

When you can
    you follow the flow

Full head of white hair
    three thousand jô[87]

Eightieth autumn of your remaining years

    With great compassion for his home
    Pliancy and patience for his robe
    The voidness of myriad dharmas for his seat
    Abiding in these, he preaches the Law

        [Hokkekyô, (*Lotus Sutra*) Hoshibon chapter]

Kûgyoku (Final Emptiness)

What is the seat of the myriad dharmas?

In the ten directions
    not a speck of dust

Destroy this mind
    and you reach the ground of no-mind

Penetrating to the place where Buddhas are chosen

---

87. A line taken from Li Po's verse. Li Po grieves his painful years. Here Jakushitsu is expressing a feeling of the acceptance of aging. A jô is approximately ten feet.

SHÔOKU (WOODCUTTER'S HOUSE)

1

You cut down a blossoming tree
    and a withering tree
        with a single stroke

Carry them back to your hut
    by the mountain stream

No buyer to sell them to

You shut your brushwood gate
    and sleep in the mist and smoke

2

Ax hanging from your waist
    you carry withered firewood home

Your reed hut
    by a mountain stream of course

Like the patriarch Lu
    making regular trips to Hsin-chou[88]

Gate enclosed by cold clouds
    sun sinks in the west

---

88. Lu, who was to become the Six Patriarch, sold firewood in Hsin-chou to support his mother before meeting the Fifth Patriarch.

Question: What is the Buddha dharma in the Venerable Abbot's mountain life?

Answer: In the mountains, large rocks are large, small ones are small.

[Hsi-tsung Tao-ch'uan, quoted from the *Ching-te ch'uan-teng lu*, vol. 24]

SEKIKAN (VALLEY STREAM ROCKS)

Even rough spots are flat like a whetstone

The cool river below is clear to its depths

Large rocks
    small rocks
        mountain's carefree Buddha dharma

Flooding forth busily
    a flowing transmission

Question: Don't the Three Vehicles and twelve divisions
           of teachings manifest Buddha-nature?

Master: This weed patch lies unattended.

[*Record of Lin-chi*]

KETSUDŌ (EXCELLENT SHRINE ROOM)

Your way surpasses those of ten thousand men

Tall wild autumn grasses in a desolate garden

You've reached the "falling away of the precious"[89] stage
     rare in Zen

Lanterns and pillars smile a smile
     not easily restrained

INKEI (HIDDEN VALLEY)

How many springs and autumns
     have you concealed the light
          and chipped away the splendor?

From the valley's river bottom
     ripped reeds
          for a roof over your head

You fear that worldly folk may try to find your dwelling?

Better not let the leaves float downstream

---

89. One of Ts'ao-shan's "Three types of falling away." The three are the falling
away of ascetics, the falling away of the precious, and the falling away accord-
ing to kind. See Cleary, *Timeless Spring*, (Tokyo: Weatherhill, 1980), pp. 52-53.

GYOKUGAN (JEWELED CRAG)

Illuminating ten thousand mountains
    not a speck of imperfection

Clear and vivid in every direction
    and tall and cold

Even the pearl worth castles
    is not out of reach

Hanging from a cliff
    why not let go!

Nowadays, there are Zen masters in excess,
but I can't find a truly foolish man.

[Nan-ch'uan P'u-yuan;
Ching-te ch'uan-teng lu, vol. 28]

GUIN (FOOLISH HERMIT)

Talent discarded
    wisdom wiped away
        you return to foolishness

No desire to leave traces of bungling
    to a world of dust

Fa-ch'ang moved his reed hut to a more secluded spot

Liang-kung entered the western mountain
    carrying his staff

A monk asked Pai-chang: What is the most wonderful
thing in the world?

The master answered: That I am sitting alone on
Ta-hsing Peak.

[Wu, *The Golden Age of Zen*, p. 92]

MORIN (OVERGROWN FOREST)

Deep lush forest
     shade spread wide

A source of good timber
     rare quality beams and ridge poles

Reminds me of the monastery
     established on Ta-hsing Peak

Spreading cool shade around the world
     clarifying the ways of the ancients

A monk asked Ta-lung:	"Since the body decomposes, what is the indestructible dharma body?"[90]
Ta-lung responded:	"Flowers bloom, covering the mountain like brocade. The valley stream is deep like indigo."

[*Pi-yen lu,* Case 82]

IKKAN (ONE VALLEY STREAM)

Original vessel
    how can it fall
        to the secondary
            to the tertiary

Don't ford a tributary of verbiage

Don't you know that which doesn't mix with the common flow

Without a drop
    its color resembles indigo

---

90. The dharma body, or dharmakaya, is one of the three bodies in Buddhology. The three bodies are the nirmānkāya, apparitional body; the sambhogakāya, enjoyment body (idealized, perfected form personified); and the dharmakāya, the cosmic body of the Buddha (the absolute and consummate reality of the Buddha). See Demoulin, *Zen Buddhism: A History,* vol. 1, p.3.

A special transmission outside the scriptures
Not founded upon words and letters;
By pointing directly to [one's] mind
It lets one see into [one's own true] nature and
[thus] attain Buddhahood.

> [Tsu-t'ing shih-yuan. See Demoulin,
> *Zen Buddhism: A History*, vol. 1, p. 85]

FURYŪ (NONDEPENDENCE)

Who affirms?
    who denies?

Cast all aside
    emptiness
        will freely manifest

Rows of wild geese
    inscribe characters
        in the autumn evening sky

Unexpected
    our sect defiled

JŌCHŪ (AMIDST QUIET)

I sit quietly alone
    in a room

Absolutely nothing outside to disturb my composure

Yet once I thought to cut the bamboo by my window

Ears rattled by wind on its branches
    rain on its leaves

JIKIÔ (STRAIGHTFORWARD OLD MAN)

I point to the person
  to make him see into his own nature
    and I'm still meandering

If my father steals a sheep
  would I speak out against him?[91]

The fellow from the backwoods
  white hair shaking about

Who loves his farm work
  and his mulberry leaf picking
    can do better than that!

GUMOKU (FOOLISH SILENCE)

When I have absolutely no ability
  my mind's already ash

Hungry I eat
  thirsty I drink
    freely foolish

Though my mouth
  received from my mother
    is tightly shut

Who would listen anyway
  to its roaring thunder sound?

---

91. In *The Analects*, Confucius uses the example of the boy speaking out against his father as an example of what you should not do. Jakushitsu seems to be using the quote in the opposite sense.

ZŌSŌ (VENERABLE TREASURE STORE)

Just as the light of the *mani* pearl was hidden

I've secluded myself from the world
>how many times have greens turned yellow?

Unconcerned that neither demons nor Buddhas
>can easily find my whereabouts

My white locks flutter in the autumn wind
>I meditate under a setting sun

Ta-mei (Great Plum) asked Ma-tsu: What is Buddha?

Ma-tsu answered: This mind is Buddha.

>[*Wu-men Kuan*, case 30]

BAIZAN (PLUM MOUNTAIN)

Last night flowers opened
>on a single branch
>>staving off the snow

Spring returns
>to a thousand crags
>>ten thousand peaks

To ponder the meaning:
>"This mind is Buddha"

Face the tallest peak
>and go forward

SHUNKOKU (SPRING VALLEY)

Clouds envelope peach flowers
    hang over cave entrance

As though calling
    as though responding
        the confused cry of a bush warbler

Wind and light of an eternal spring

Scenic Ching-chou Valley in Mount Lu
    only brings a mocking smile to my face

HŌGAI (BEYOND BOUNDARIES)

Genuine dwelling for a truly grounded monk

Beyond the limits of the worlds in six directions

How pitiful!
    Even the successive generations of patriarchs

Found it difficult to leave India and China

In Hua District of Hsiu Province the priest Ch'uan-tzu had
been a ferry boatman for thirty years. One of his poems
was as follows:

> A thousand meters of silk thread
> hanging straight down
> One wave moves a bit
> Ten thousand waves follow

A government official asked Ch'uan-tzu: "Revered priest,
what is your daily activity?"

Ch'uan-tzu responded: "The boat pole penetrates pure
waves, but rarely makes contact with golden scales."

*Ch'uan-tzu finally met a superior man, Lai-shan Shan-hui,
and remarked:* "My hook exhausted the inlet waves and
finally made contact with golden scales."

[*Wu-teng hui-yuan*, vol. 5]

CHÔGETSU (CATCHING THE MOON)

From a small craft
    I drop my line many fathoms

How often have I aimed for golden scales?

Tonight I didn't take the boat pole in vain

The reflection of the moon moved
    and I hooked it with my barb

TÔIN (HIDDEN PEACH)

Empty cave
    locked in mist

Crimson peach blossom
    brings joy to my aloneness

Even those who fled the tyrant Ch'in
    can't enter

Setting sun
    flowing stream
        how many springs has the wind blown in?

MUKÔ (NO AFFIRMATION)

I hate the sound of the word *Buddha*

I have little regard for *Zen of the patriarchs*

None of the many dharmas touches my heart

I simply face the green mountains
    pillow puffed high
        and nap

Virtuous monks, understand he who plays with these
reflections. He is the origin of all the Buddhas. Wherever
the follower of the Way returns is his home.

[*Record of Lin-chi*]

FOR BLIND ZESSHÔ (BEYOND ILLUMINATION)

In daily practice
    can one who plays with reflections

Ever attain the Way?

Smash the worthless old mirror

And your original face will shine

The World-Honored-One transmitted the True Dharma
Eye to Mahâkâshyapa at Vulture Peak. I would say this is
nothing other than talking of the moon. Ts'ao-hsi, the
Sixth Patriarch, lifted his whisk (pointing to people's
minds). This too is just the finger pointing at the moon.

[Hsuan-sha Shih-pei, from the
Ching-te ch'uan-teng lu, vol. 18]

GEPPÔ (MOON OVER THE PEAK)

The talk at Vulture Peak
    the finger of Ts'ao-hsi

Nothing more than daily reflections

Fix your eyes mightily on the eminent

And you will penetrate the moon
    on the lone peak of the Unknown

ZUIGAN (CONGRATULATORY CRAG)

Mushrooms
   like bright jewels
      sprouting from a crag

Steep precipice
   reaching halfway to the sky

Last night
   a lone monkey
      cried in the moonlight

Each cry sounded like
   "Master!"[92]

T'ai-yuan lectured on the dharma-body (Truth-body) from
the Nirvana Sutra at the Kuang-hsiao Temple in the
Chinese province of Yang. At the end of the lecture, he
noticed a Zen man chuckling. T'ai-yuan asked him why he
was chuckling. The Zen man told him to stop lecturing for
ten days and to sit quietly, emptying his mind. He did so
and on the fifth watch of the first night (between 4 and 6
A.M.) he heard the sound of a horn and was enlightened.

[*Wu-teng hui-yuan*, vol. 7]

TAIGEN (NOBLE ORIGIN)

In ancient times there lived a priest

Who after lecturing on the "Truth-body"
   returned to his home

A single note from a horn
   carried by the wind
      and

How many blossoms fell
   from winter plum branches?

---

92. See above p. 1.

In the great town of Vaisâli there lived an elder named Vimalakîrti. He had shown respect to leaders of the past, made offerings to countless Buddhas, and had deeply planted good roots, thereby achieving an understanding of the Unborn...

At that point, Manjusrî said to Vimalakîrti: "We have all stated our understanding of the non-dual Dharma; please give us yours."

Then, Vimalakîrti, mouth shut tight, remained silent.

At that, Manjusrî exclaimed: "Excellent, excellent."

[*The Vimalakirti Nirdesa Sutra*]

MOKUSAI (SILENT OFFERING)

Like the old master of Vaisâli
    his mouth shut

Silent and alone
    all day long
        gate closed

The good news
    should not be spread
        frivolously

That valley stream and mountain
    beyond those eaves
        talk too much

UNKAN (CLOUDS AND A VALLEY STREAM)

You return to this valley stream
    enveloping moss-covered stones

As though regretting having ever left that mountain cave

From now on
    you will live a quiet leisurely existence

While the stream flows busily by

CHÔUN (CLOUD CLUSTER)

One hundred million scattered fragments
    become a massive cluster

How can this mass float effortlessly
    separating from the summit?

It now covers Mount Niu-t'ou
    lingering alone
        eternally at ease

Welcomed by Patriarch Jan[93]
    his door left half ajar

---

93. Hsiao-jan from Mount Niu-t'ou.

KŌGAN (LOFTY CRAG)

Crag! Crag!
    reaching for the blue sky

Clear in all directions
    higher and higher

Smoke and mist can't float so high

Sun and moon become uncertain
    circling the mountainside

Its enough now just to look
    as in antiquity

How can anyone dare to climb?

Buddhas and patriarchs simply view it and turn back

Not even Subhūti allows himself to meditate there

Man of the Way you strive to reach the sky

I take this crag and create a name

It truly matches the essence that is you

In all heaven and earth you have no equal

The world is full of impure hearts

People spending their days chasing the mean and the base

When will I return
    to see the mountain birds
        drop flowers?

With whom will I listen
    to the voice of the lone monkey
        crying to the moon?

VISITING THE PRIEST'S QUARTERS AT SEIHANZAN

A thousand peaks
    seen in one sweeping glance

Arm in arm we frolic
    climbing to heights of the southern sky

Leisurely walking through deep fog
    and violets and greens

We step on fallen leaves
    on a pebbled path
        and continue on our way

Old temple building
    deserted mountain
        cold autumn day

Steps of earth
    from continuing rain
        carpeted with moss

I'm reminded of Priest Nan-yueh
    drinking up Buddhas
        and viewing the Milky Way

Who moves to a hut now
    deep in this mountain?

This path is disdained by people these days

The song of wind through the pines ceases
    leaves shed tears of dew

My final years
    a quiet life
        and carefree mind

Let me call to the monkeys and birds
    and greet them

Show me how you will swallow the thorny chestnut shell?

[Yang-chi Fang-hui, from the
Wu-teng hui-yuan, vol. 19]

PRESENTED TO E JISHA ON HIS HOMECOMING

Your Zen training complete

Facing backward astride an iron horse
    you gallop toward the void

Not only do you dismiss swarthy Tao-an[94]
    the peerless monk

You startle Mount Sumeru into performing a back flip

I at eighty
    old and decrepit
        a hundred shortcomings

Can't believe that talented you
    would join me

Our lineage
    fortunate to have one so virtuous

Maintaining principles through adversity

You make the worthy Yang-chi's kôan
    "Thorny chestnut shell" your own

In the future
    you'll give others the drink

That India's Twenty-eighth Patriarch and China's Sixth[95]
    couldn't taste

---

94. A learned Chinese monk of the fourth century. See Demoulin, *Zen
Buddhism: A History*, pp. 66 and 67.

95. Bodhidharma is India's Twenty-eighth Patriarch, and Hui-neng is China's
Sixth.

How shall I bear the separation
    as you descend this mountain?

I stand alone
    staff in hand
        in the mountain air

Don't stay away too long
    weaving sandals for a living

Knock again on my brushwood door
    and visit me in old age